Coyote Goes Global

A Modern Journey of
Forgotten Ways

First published by O Books, 2009
O Books is an imprint of John Hunt Publishing Ltd., The Bothy, Deershot Lodge, Park Lane, Ropley, Hants, SO24 0BE, UK
office1@o-books.net
www.o-books.net

Distribution in:

UK and Europe
Orca Book Services
orders@orcabookservices.co.uk
Tel: 01202 665432 Fax: 01202 666219
Int. code (44)

USA and Canada
NBN
custserv@nbnbooks.com
Tel: 1 800 462 6420 Fax: 1 800 338 4550

Australia and New Zealand
Brumby Books
sales@brumbybooks.com.au
Tel: 61 3 9761 5535 Fax: 61 3 9761 7095

Far East (offices in Singapore, Thailand, Hong Kong, Taiwan)
Pansing Distribution Pte Ltd
kemal@pansing.com
Tel: 65 6319 9939 Fax: 65 6462 5761

South Africa
Alternative Books
altbook@peterhyde.co.za
Tel: 021 555 4027 Fax: 021 447 1430

Design: Stuart Davies

ISBN: 978 1 84694 178 8

A CIP catalogue record for this book is available from the British Library.

Printed by Digital Book Print

Coyote Goes Global

A Modern Journey of
Forgotten Ways

Star Blanket & Dream Weaver

Cover art by Sabine Baeckmann-Elge

Illustrations by Jen Upchurch

BOOKS

Winchester, UK
Washington, USA

CONTENTS

Dedication

For our Ancestors, of Spirit and Blood relations, that sacrificed so that this knowledge may come awake in our lifetime

ACKNOWLEDGMENTS

To the inspiration that was given when we were at a plateau, to find a way to write this story from multiple places, Coyote spoke through these people to assist us in fulfilling this dream:

To Susie Arnett, who brought fresh insights, helping communicate this journey, and asking the questions that irritated and challenged the integrity of the teachings.

To Zhena, who completed the editing process from an Elder perspective.

To Sabine, we thank our new friend for patiently supporting us in developing the cover art.

To Jen Upchurch, for her determination and willingness to lend her artistic talent to creating the illustrations.

To all of the students, clients, and Seekers that helped bring the ancient knowledge out and into the light.

We want to thank all of our friends and family who brought a mirror of reflection whether it was inspiring or challenging, or both! Thank you to Barry and Susan Gordon for helping launch the research of the Awakened Water. To Thunderbird Star Woman for the daily visits, assisting learning to write and Keeping a Medicine Way perspective. To our new friend, Chandra Porter, for helping us open up another trail of discovery. To Frank Stronghorse for his willingness to explore the depths and challenges of the Warrior paradigm. To Whirlwind and Star Trees for providing the Elder perspective from our Lineage and providing their continued love of these ways.

From Star Blanket:

To my sons, Jacob, Micah, and Ian, and all youth of the planet that we've left this unknown future too, we hope that the writing of this book will leave some trail to follow and we would hope that someday we will all know the perfection of the challenges that we are leaving them to face.

To cousin Keith for always believing in my path.

To Cricket for your support and love you have shown in writing the study manuals.

To Crystal Pathfinder for always being available to consult and ready to be with the land.

To my parents who prepared the way with a farming lifestyle and finding sobriety. I am learning what you went through with risk taking children. Thank you.

To Dream Weaver, you are truly a friend and comrade. Thank you for being willing to risk being yourself with a delicate subject and traditional value system. Our journey's together will always be precious and inspirational. Words are inadequate to express my gratitude.

From Dream Weaver:

To Jeanne, who has opened my heart as we journey together while walking all of the qualities of truth in a Beauty Way.

To my parents, who realized that they were raising a Free Dancer from an early age and encouraged that journey with as much beauty, grace, and love as any child could have ever hoped for in this lifetime.

To Eagle Star Blanket, for all of your infinite wisdom and mastery of these ways that you humbly share with me on a daily basis and that you continually share with all Four Worlds. I have great gratitude for all of the moments we share and spend together.

For additional information regarding teachings, lodges, cyclic readings and events visit Braided Traditions at http://www.braidedtraditions.com or email at info@braidedtraditions.com

Introduction

Conifer, Colorado USA 2007 A.D.

"Everything is related"

When out of balance, a correction must follow; Nature is the only force that humbles Humanity during its quest for immortality. Visionaries and Prophets have spoken of the days when Mother life would correct the global illusions of Power. The legend is alive again and on the prowl.

Coyote is a legend, myth and symbolic spirit that has been the main character around many a campfire. The tales have been passed on by role playing, stories, visions or viewing Coyote in the wild. This ultimate survivor lives the paradoxes of life as an explorer, hunter, thrill seeker and trickster. As a trickster, Coyote is the spirit that can turn things up side down or right side up depending on the mood. In either situation the results usually spin a scenario towards balance.

Coyote was chosen as the character for this tale, because of Coyote's relentless pursuit to prove how important he or she is. How does this relate to everyday life circumstances? Humans often are relentless to prove how important they are. This undercurrent has been the motivation for many conquests and wars, whether by the sword, gun or pen. Like a Coyote, humans often trick themselves into a myth of deserving more than others. We would also hope that world leaders would be able to laugh with us as we look at ourselves through this lens.

The current global supply of resources for life is under siege and corrections are predicted by many humans and other species. Our story and teachings are intended to connect global events with individual human journeys to wholeness. To do so, we are taking the personal journey of Dream Weaver, a high tech guru of sorts, as she is tutored by Star Blanket in the teachings of Nature's

Ways. During this river of learning, many experiences of her services to a global network are reflections of her own lessons to master. Coyote becomes the teacher often tricking her into her shining. This tale is based upon a true story in a historical fiction way.

The knowledge represented here is from many circles that Guy Gilleshammer AKA Lone Eagle or Star Blanket has discovered from the roots of being Métis, who live in North Dakota USA and Canada, to South America and many areas in between. The knowledge in this book does not represent any organized religion, spiritual tradition or path of study. The knowledge is a woven braid from the quests for wholeness of Lone Eagle as shared with comrades, students, seekers and apprentices. Coyote is the spirit guide on the trail which offers an honoring to all past and present storytellers, who kept the legend and purpose alive.

The Métis are often defined as a forgotten people in northern regions of North America. Other forgotten people from other regions use terms like Sami, Mestizo, or Mulatto. All terms are used to represent Mixed Bloods that have fallen into the gaps of societies and they share the purpose of claiming their rights within traditional bloodlines and cultural standards. The common symbol of Braids connects these peoples in what we call Braided Traditions.

Coyote Goes Global brings the wisdom of the Braided Traditions as a way of remembering that everything is related. It's a tradition where diverse threads of ancient and contemporary knowledge of Nature's Ways are braided together. The purpose is to create a united Truth that can illuminate more integrated ways of living in harmony with the everything.

The Forgotten People

History reveals that an exploration of the new world (North America) occurred in the 14th and 15th centuries when the Norse tried settling in the eastern shores of Canada and the United

States. Many cultures throughout the Americas experienced a similar history. The mixing of culture, knowledge, music, and religions became progressively unavoidable as intermarriages occurred. Distinctive nations and cultures of the Mixed Bloods solidified in the history of North America, Central America and South America after explorers returned with stories of the untold wealth of the new land and claimed the territory for their respective monarchs and countries.

The word "MÉTIS" comes from the Latin "miscere", meaning "to mix"; and was used originally to describe the children of Indian mothers and European fathers. Another term for the Métis is derived from the Ojibwa (Indians) word wissakodewinmi, which means "half-burnt woodsmen", describing their lighter complexion in comparison to that of full-blood Indians.

The Métis are a mixed blood people, the joining of the old world (Europeans) and the new world (North American Indians). However, historic records show that the Métis were often overlooked, exploited or deprived of their rights.

The common misconception is that the Métis practiced only the religion of their fathers (Catholicism or Protestant). The truth is that like the Métis Nation itself, the spiritual mixture is as complex as the people who make up the nation.

From the beginning, the Métis child absorbed the teachings of both father and mother. Those teachings were made up of the Father's religious background and the traditional teachings of the Aboriginal Nation of the Mother. The children learned to live in both the Aboriginal and White worlds encompassing both into their spirituality.

This ability to learn from all of the nations they came in contact with added to the future spirituality of the Métis. Today Métis practice all forms of religion, from mainline Christianity to New Age concepts and everything in between. From their Catholicism, they have the Patron Saint of Métis People, St. Joseph of Nazareth. From their Aboriginal Relatives they incorporate the sweat lodge, medicine wheel, sacred pipe and Long House ceremonies, and many other Aboriginal spiritual practices.

Many Métis People, as with other Aboriginal communities, have lost their spiritual connections to the past because of marginalization or poverty and decimation of their communities and their way of life. The healing has begun and the renewal of their spirituality is an exciting journey that many Métis People are taking. It is very common to encounter a prayer and a smudge at the opening and closing of meetings of Métis People.

The Métis were the trailblazers who led explorers, missionaries and traders westward and inland. They acted as middlemen between advancing European settlement and the Indian bands. They acted as interpreters when treaties with Indians were negotiated. They brought the Province of Manitoba into being and fought against the annexation of the North West Territories to the United States. These contributions have often been ignored by traditional ancestors who used their own land base for credibility. Today, all the Métis seek is restitution and the recognition due to them for their role in building these nations.

Like Coyote, Mixed Bloods often have repeating experiences until memories are clear and or the learning cycle is complete. The most focused humans will find paths of study and discipline to open memories and reveal the teaching. Often these Seekers experience alienation from society, family and other forms of regulated rules of morality. This is their strength and weakness. It is a paradoxical puzzle. They will eventually embody the medicine of Coyote.

After many years of providing spiritual healing, many revelations of how interrelatedness exists have been shown to Star Blanket. In the human energy fields, Star Blanket often sees patterns throughout the aura and energy body that record the many life experiences of that individual. The visual symbol usually looks like a string of beads, or a long hair with dots on it weaving throughout the energy field like a spider's web. Each bead or dot represents a set of life experiences from the current or past incarnations.

The bead-like dots are intervals or plateaus on a timeline of continuing evolution. They record in the energy field as a closed or open system. If the experience is closed the stream of remembering cannot pass through and that's where Star Blanket focuses during the healing session. Once the beads opens, the life force energy can pass through it. It, and the area, will cleanse itself. If already open these intervals are feeding the wisdom to the consciousness of that person. The teaching here is that there is a weaving of the patterns in the body that creates a linkage to The Everything that exists. The opening of these closed beads of memory is the intended goal of this tale on a global scale. Coyote will assist us.

Who are we?

We, the writers, embody Braided Traditions and you can know this because we are hyphenates. Hyphenates are living proof of the power of braiding disparate knowledge into a new form in order to create wholeness in a fragmented world.

Dream Weaver is a software engineer-high-tech consultant-student of the shamanic ways. The singularity of her results-oriented, driven lifestyle in the high-tech field was destroying her. Plagued by migraines and conflict, she sought out another thread to braid into her existing pool of knowledge to expand her consciousness. She found it as an apprentice of the Shamanic Arts.

Star Blanket is a Shaman. He was born into a farming family in North Dakota and has combined his studies in esoteric knowledge, religion, and Ceremony with a deep, ancestral understanding of the rhythm and truth of the land, plants, and animals.

This book is a living tale of their shared journey as they search for an understanding of the Forces at work in all of our lives. We uncover teachings from many different cultures that date back thousands of years. These include years of teaching lodges, mystery schools, journeys, experiences and counseling sessions. Some of the teachings and prophecies have never before been made public.

In this book, we examine the cause of the current imbalances that exist on an individual and collective level. By 'out of balance' we mean that more is being taken than given, from Mother Earth, from our relationships, from ourselves.

Humans are in a constant state of entitlement. By interfacing the legend of Coyote with personal lives, the humor of our pursuit may be revealed. The progression of current lifestyles won't change over night. The goal of balance and personal accountability offers a new approach to an ageless and faceless pattern. The capitalist and opportunist approach is dying with the lack of global resources.

Coyote Goes Global is a play on words. Coyote represents 'Trickster-Medicine', meaning that fantasies and illusions will be exposed in unexpected ways. Many of us have bought into our own "slavery", in forms that are totally acceptable by modern standards. Upon closer examination, we will see how this is true and we'll learn ways to become free.

We approach this writing with a global perspective and individual attitude. Each and every human adds a collective unity to this writing. Once again our hope is to illuminate reflections of how personal journeys reflect the whole and the whole reflects back to the individual. We will show how answers are in Nature. Nature has no judgment, no right or wrong. Nature has a justice by which it functions. We strive as Seekers to learn from this type of teacher and to share what we learn with you. By looking and seeing to Nature, we have found mirrors of our own souls.

When reading in a Shamanic Braided Tradition, many insights about your own journey may be revealed. The teachings may come at different speeds and times. Some may be layered in masks of diversion and others so blatant that you will have to laugh. This is the way of Coyote. You will know that the answers are on their way, by the recognition of events that show up. Our hope is that the journey is honorable.

Be wise in your choices.

Prologue

Colorado, USA 2005 A.D.

Star Blanket:

The night sweats had dwindled in frequency the last couple of weeks and the voices were very quiet. It was almost eerie. I had been through six major passages since the day Deer had given me a spirit heart in 1983. That day occurred twenty-one years ago. This last passage of fifteen months had been the most intense. Maybe because it was fresh I thought to myself. As I lay in bed, I looked out the window to see 20 inches of fresh snow covering everything. It was warmer to stay right here under the covers.

As I lay back to dream some more, my attention drifted back through the last fifteen months. The Elders had called it a pregnancy because I was birthing my Elder for which I'd been given the name Star Blanket. This passage required a death of my male ego to a degree that scared me every night. For most of my initiation, I had been reluctant to go to bed. The voices always started at about 11 p.m. I would lay awake, or what seemed like being awake for five to six hours each night. I was in many dreams, always with hundreds of spirits talking at once and always Grandmother sitting at the edge of the bed translating. She would say that I had to be taught to remember the council.

As I watched the snow continue, I knew she was referring to one of two councils. One was learned when studying in Arizona. It was a council of Twisted Hairs around 1224 A.D. in Mexico. The other was one Grandfather Eagleheart had spoken about where totems from around the world were represented. I was only given pieces of both, but there was enough to spark the dreaming and awaken some deep memory. I knew the next year would involve integrating the visions that I had reclaimed over the last fifteen months. Many had been given. One was of the healing powers of Water. Another had been an all night affair about the folks that would find me now. They would all be searching for the memories I had just claimed. They would sense it around me, but would not know what they were attracted to. This was going to be an interesting time of my life I thought as the snow seduced me back into a sleep. My last thought was, "How crazy this is. There is no difference between the day and the night. It is all connected."

First Council of Renewal

Upper Michigan around 720 A.D.

Buffalo Heart:

The winter was beginning its long nights. I sat around the campfire stretching my legs. The round cabin nearby with its mud packing would be warmer, but this night I wanted to be under the stars. Power was in the air. My nostrils burned with excitement as the cold tried to mask the intensity. Winter was approaching. I lived in what would be called upper Michigan. Campfires dotted the valley along with homes, tipis and some earthen lodges. I was called Buffalo Heart and I had come to be the local Medicine Man despite being a half-breed. The days preceding this star filled evening had been quiet, as power crept in to my veins.

Two strangers approached the village and were exchanging words with a campfire down the hill, a couple of stones throw from where I sat. I saw glances come my way and knew the time had come. I had been meeting several Dreamers in the metaphysical realms as of late. This was not unusual for my work, however this time, there were many different colors of people and images from other lands that I had only seen in symbolic writings on bark and cave walls. The strangers began walking my way, which was tradition and they gestured loudly waiting for a signal that it was okay to approach. They knew it was not good to approach if I was in a dream. I saw that they were a man and woman when the fire cast its light upon their faces.

After greetings and traditional gifts of tobacco were given the woman with white skin of 30 some summers began to speak. "We have come from where the great rivers meet and have traveled far to find you. We are here to deliver this package." She began unwrapping a deer hide with a bladder bag inside. It was filled with water. The young woman said, "The Medicine Woman with Fired Water said you would know what to do with it. She also said

I should draw this symbol in the dirt. If you recognize the symbol you will continue to visit with us."

She picked up a stick out of the fire and drew a circle in the dirt. She paused and noted no response from me. She continued and drew a horizontal and vertical line that crossed in the center of the circle. Then she reached into her pouch and withdrew four smaller pouches. The first one was yellow corn meal. She outlined one quarter of the circle, and then she reached for another pouch of red stone powder. She continued, outlining another quarter of the circle. The next pouch was black lightning powder from a tree that had been charred. She outlined another quarter. The last pouch was white sand and she finished the circle. It was exactly as it had been in my dream. They were true messengers.

I instructed them to camp nearby and I would council with them in four days. After they left my campfire, I sent word to the encampment and my three apprentices that I was not to be disturbed. The apprentices were to prepare a morning lodge. They would also attend to my needs of food and water. I would begin with the new day's birthing. The Sweat Lodge would open the doorways to the dream. It had begun!

Dawn was magnificent with red and orange as I arose after four days of dreaming and drinking the coded water. The assemblage of Dreamers would be happening in one year. Steps would be taken to seed the future. It would take me 2 months of travel to reach my destination. I would be gone for a full sun cycle. My apprentices would take over my duties. They were ready. The two strangers and 6 helpers would take me by canoe on the river in the spring to where the great rivers crossed. I would meet others and council there.

Fork of Two Great Rivers

Our group of 20 arrived a few weeks before the winter solstice. The journey had been long. There were six Dreamers in our group. We had traveled by boat south on the great river. Other

Dreamers had joined our party along the way. The last adventure was across the plains to the land of ceremonial temples. Skinner, our captain and guide, had been chosen for his outstanding leadership and respect for Dreamers. He always knew when to visit and when to stay away, like when we were in spirit realms. The riders had become friends and were going to witness the event. They would record it in a secret way. The site was chosen for several reasons. The location was mixed with people, cultures and religions. The local people were not threatened by large ceremonies even though they would not be allowed to attend. People from around the world were gathering.

It was one week before the winter solstice and many mini councils were randomly taking place as Dreamers and other visionaries exchanged dream time stories, symbols and wisdom. It felt like a homecoming in many ways, except the Ceremony of Fire Seeding had not been done for several centuries. I walked around as the sun was setting. The astrological medicine wheel was huge. It could hold four to five hundred people.

Towards the south there was a trail and I knew at once that it led to the Cave of Testing. Inside would be initiation ceremonies with ancient symbols and crystals. Only the most developed of all the folks would come out with a "look". The "look" would grant them passage through the portals to provide the Fire Seeding. I looked to the east of the wheel where the campfires began their dance as the sun went down the mountain of foliage. It was well planned. Some of us would not return from this journey and others would lose their lives upon returning home. The physical death was a courageous trade for keeping the knowledge alive since visions predicted a future of wars, disease and the destruction of Nature's Ways. This Fire Seeding would protect the wisdom until a future generation was ready to re-awaken to happiness and harmony. We all knew the risks and knew that weaving our wisdom and principles for social and magical order was the only option to preserve Earth's resources. Two days left. I would be ready!

I felt the tension each day as the trusting bond was building for the Ceremony. The crack in the veils of time would be available during the solstice. The goal was to dream through that doorway and place a sphere of energy that could hold its integrity of intent into Spirit's hands. It would be encoded with collective intents for the time when the inhabitants of Earth would begin the stages of coexisting. These days of material acquisitions would come to an end. The codes would also contain a plan for the delegation to certain species on Earth to carry out the activating of the codes. Others would grow the seeds of intent.

The many colors of people and styles of dress created no separation as the first Council prepared to begin. The area was glowing with wisdom from many countries. Weaving the wisdom into symbolic braids was going to be easy. The braid was a common symbol through all cultures represented. Baskets, sweet grass, hats, tobacco and clothes all had symbolic art of braiding. In the Dream-time we already set up most of the intents. Now we would council to join the intents of spirit with the substance of Earth. This would create a song throughout the universe to distribute and regulate the codes of intent.

The evening arrived about an hour before dusk. We assembled in a large circle as Skinner and other group guardians outlined the protocols for speaking. We would not begin the council talk until after dark. Being in the firelight was a universal custom so no one was intimidated by facial expressions and body language. This also allowed the link between the day and night. The fire would burn in place of the sun.

I left the circle just before dawn. It had been grueling and exciting. It was decided that the Circle would be our foundational map. The element of water would be placed in the south. Air in the north. The wheels we created would lay on top of each other to mark the trail that we had journeyed and would be like a Tribal Tree encoded for any Seekers to find their way into the wisdom.

Animals, plants and minerals would be placed on wheels for their signature medicines for people's discovery of the encrypted codes.

As I walked to my bedroll and prepared for the dream, one discussion played over and over in my head; Trickster, trickster, trickster. Every culture represented at this council had a trickster in their social lives. Whether human, animal and sometimes both, it was clear that the tricksters were going to be cut loose in the spirit world when the timing was right. I almost started giggling at the thought. Then it hit me like a slap on the face. Coyote howled like a thunderous boom. Old Coyote, the survivor of every change in stories the old ones told, could make it through the passages of change and still carry the codes. It fit.

My sleep was interrupted by a beautiful song. I slowly peeked out of my bed-roll and saw the Sweat Lodge fire. They were almost ready. I relieved myself behind some bush like trees with only a hide covering my loins. By the time I walked to the lodge site, the providers of the Ceremony were ready with smudge and a drink of water. The water had some roots in it for stamina. I entered the lodge with other Elders.

The day was dreamy and I had to stay awake for the Cave of Testing. I kept alert by playing with some stones along a steam. Different folks were being called at random times for the test. There was no pecking order between Dreamers, Dancers, Scientists, Warriors or Scouts. All would be given the test, an initiatic test to determine their skill level and heart for the future. At mid afternoon a short man with big smile came over and handed me a horn from a Buffalo. It was my time. He would be my monitor.

The entrance opened behind some huge plants. It was secluded from any one passing by. Near the entrance there were pools of water that had gathered from the rains. I leaned down and blessed myself with a drink and then splashed my face until spirit filled my cheeks. I entered. My monitor stayed behind. The walls had writings and symbols that flickered life with the torches that lit the path.

I walked until a large room opened up before me. There was a pool of hot water in the center. I knew at once to shed my loin cloth and walk into the water. Once I settled in I began to look around. Three attendants were quietly watching me as I looked above. The concave shaped ceiling walls were all crystalline needles pointing at the water. As I merged with the wall of needles, a drum began a heartbeat rhythm that echoed through the cave passages. Lightning bolts began streaming out of the crystal needles into the water. As the water heated up, I entered the dream where there was no separation. I was the lightning and crystal needles. I became the water and the heartbeat. I was no more.

I awoke in my bedroll. It was dark and the drumbeat had started to announce the Ceremony of Fire Seeding. I prepared myself in a Robe of the Buffalo. It was very hot but I was also representing my people, and many knew this symbol back in upper Michigan. They would be praying for me while dancing and drumming to send power my way. The robe would collect the extra energy. I walked to the entrance of the Medicine Wheel. I had passed the test and a position was given for me to sit in. Those who did not pass the test would dance and chant from around the outside of the circle. Drum beats and chants from every culture there would be heard this night. Nobody was excluded from the faith they had showed by coming to this council.

The Fire Seeding Ceremony had been successful. I was resting which was required during each day. Nightly discussions continued after the Ceremony. Councils would be taking place each evening for another four days before many groups would depart for their homelands. Some folks would stay and tend to the ceremonial grounds until all the image of the Fire Seeding Ceremony evaporated. This would take three moons or eighty-four days.

It had been two days since the Fire Seeding Ceremony. The "Return" had set in to all participants and it was crucial that we all get through it successfully before returning home. Spirit was going as deep inside the body as it had traveled outside. Images, memories and emotions that lay deep within would be dislodged and examined. If the old imprints still served, then spirit would keep it. If not it would be released. This time is Coyote's favorite playground. My nap was restless this day as the "Return" had set in. My mind was busy as I tried to convince my body to rest.

Weaver came by bringing hot water with roots for the dreamtime. The name had been given to her during the Ceremony. This day she was wearing a multi-colored cloth around her head to keep her hair from blowing in her face. It seemed that every council fire she attended, another colorful article would be added to her person. Weaver never stopped asking questions. It was obvious that she was gathering the knowledge as fast as she could. The spirit world must have been watching when the name was given. After drinking the hot nourishing tea I returned to my nap and was soon traveling.

I watched the vision before me like a bear watching her cub. A sphere of intents circled the earth like a small moon. The small moon sphere was darkened so it was easy to see streams of light fall off the sphere into clouds. The clouds became filled with lightning and rain that would shower the land. The Fire Seeds, each filled with an intention, were being released to the natural cycles.

Water evaporated into the air during the spring and summer suns. Rains and wind distributed the water across the lands. The streams, rivers and lakes would regulate the flow through areas where the plants and animals would contribute to the distribution as well as using the water for their own growth. I watched as a Beaver built a dam for the animals to drink and bathe. The seeds were digested and absorbed into the living. The plants would release the seeds with fresh oxygen while animals passed it on by natural survival and offspring. Humans were also being given the seeds by the air and water along with the foods they ate. The vision progressed revealing natural cycles becoming altered by humans. This slowed down the awakening of the seeds, however the waters were alive or fired with the spirit seeds. In time all would be awakened. The vision blurred as the images turned to winter. I watched a similar movement with snow.

My spirit came back into my body with a sudden jerk and I jumped up in my bedroll. I looked around and remembered where I was. Looking around the encampment, I saw that many of the others were looking around too. It was like we all had the same thoughts. I saw their spirits twinkling, hiding the caution, or was that Coyote? We were not done yet.

Chapter 0 - Death

Turtle Mountains, North Dakota USA 1990 A.D.

Star Blanket:

"First learn the rules", Eagleheart said to me, as the Coleman lantern dimly glowed. It was late and the round house revealed its lengthening shadows. A committee for the upcoming Sun Dance had left an hour ago leaving Grandfather and me alone. It was the fall of 1990 and the cool air was seeping in around us. Eagleheart spoke, "You have heard the call of spirit," he continued, "the winds of spirit will never let you rest long or conform to an ordinary life."

Eagleheart deliberately and patiently continued, "The medicine path of the spirit world is a lifestyle that has challenged all Shamans, Medicine Women, Medicine Men and Sorcerers since the beginning of time as we know it. Paths of knowledge and initiations will be set before you to learn the rules of engagement, language, confronting your demons and embracing your beauty. You will learn to live with power and have faith in the Creator's ways. First learn the rules, for many are called and fall to the darkness within humanity. Never underestimate the power and allurements of the darkness."

Eagleheart shared stories for the next two hours of brothers and sisters that had faced these challenges. Then he spoke in another tone and I knew to stop dreaming and to listen carefully. "The rules are always changing. You must learn the language to understand these changes. The mastery of moving with power is shamanic science, craft and systems. Do not be fooled by fantasy and phenomenon, for the darkness preys on diversion of focus. The science is the study and knowledge of cycles and patterns. The craft is the practice of healing ways, of Ceremony, of assisting those who seek, and of teaching humans to open their hearts to the spirit of nature. The systems are the weaving of wisdom in the physical world as Sky Woman and Spider Woman work in the stars. The hills and valleys of your journey will be filled with tests to your faith. Only you can decide the path before you. If you choose the path of learning mastery, you will find the trail that leaves the forest of the mind."

With a crooked smile and gaps in his teeth, Grandfather leaned back and laughed loudly. "I don't know, there might be something to it." And with that he stood offering his hand in closing. "Follow your heart, not your pity, for the book of life of everyone is already written." With that, Eagleheart turned down the Coleman lantern and we left each other in that way.

As I drove back to Grand Forks, ND, within the Stars' Blanket, I dreamt back to 1983 when I was ready to die from lack of purpose. For years, the drugs and alcohol had numbed the pain. I remembered following my family's dream for me that had included farming, marriage and fatherhood. I remembered choosing that path, for my fear ruled my decisions. As I drove, I went back to that day — November 26th, 1983 — when I was sick from the heroin in my veins. It was 5 a.m. and I had gone to the woods carrying my bow and arrows. Twenty below zero brought the snow to a screeching siren in my head as I planned my death. Then something happened up ahead and behind a large winter bush. A loud sound of something heavy being dragged across the softened fall leaves echoed through my soul while all other thoughts faded. I turned and started to run off.

Only a few yards later I froze as the sound grew louder. I turned to see skid marks in the snow that led to another bush further ahead. My mind was wild as spirit circled my aura. I pulled my bow to a shooting position, set an arrow and began creeping slowly towards the bush. Shaking, I drew my arrow back as I rounded the corner in full sight of the skid marks. Shock filled me as I gazed upon a small deer lying under a bush with three broken legs. My mind whirled as I relaxed my grip and let off the arrow.

Tears welled in my eyes as I recalled when, a few weeks prior, on an early morning, I had raced down a gravel road trying desperately to get to my drug supplier before he took off for work. Two deer had jumped out onto the road. I hit the brakes then as my pickup went into a broad slide, striking the side of one of the deer. The deer had limped into the woods as I continued my quest for drugs. Here lay the deer I had hit. In a moment of hours I saw all the destruction I had caused from my lack of courage. Tears overwhelmed me as the spirit world invited me into its grace. The deer and I locked our gazes as a 'knowing' passed through me. I knew what to do. We were to trade spirits.

As I pulled back my bow and shot the arrow, I knew I was killing myself. The deer's spirit entered my heart at the moment of impact. I gathered up its body and left the woods that cold morning, knowing that my journey of getting sober had started. With great relief and strong support from my family and wife, I checked into a treatment center the next day.

Coming back from that memory and concentrating on the road in front of me, Eagleheart's words seemed to come alive. I thought about the work that I had done getting sober over the course of the last 7 years since I met that deer. Now, I realized my sacred journey was beginning another chapter. And I realized it was true: my book of life had already been written.

Conifer, Colorado USA 2004 A.D.

Dream Weaver:

Her arm is bruised and the tech is trying to find another vein. She winces from the pain. I do too inside. There are about 20 people around us all laying back on recliners getting chemotherapy too. It makes me think of a MASH unit or death chamber. Even the bag hanging from the IV has a skull and crossbones on it, reminding us that sometimes you have to poison yourself to get better.

She lays back. Pulling up a chair, I begin whispering in her ear.

"Breathe in health, exhale the cancer." After 13 years together as life partners, the closeness is soothing as I lead her through this meditation for the hour of the drip. It's my ritual to help her, and for me to move through this moment, as we walk through the black clouds.

A year later, I'm sitting at the back of a crowded room in the basement of a Buddhist retreat in Boulder. There are about 40 people sitting in rows on meditation cushions. Two rows up is the woman I have fallen in love with. Life has gotten very complicated.

The Lama is leading us in an old Sanskrit chant called "Moonbeams Overcoming Darkness", about purifying karma. This is hour 4 of an 8-hour chanting meditation and I'm grateful for the repetition of sounds, for the 108 syllables that are keeping my mind focused and hopefully clearing my karma from the mess I have made of my life.

"Namo ratna trayaya..."

During the break, we all walk outside. It is a beautiful, spring day. I check my phone and my partner has called 12 times. She had gone through my emails yesterday and found everything. Last night, as my new found love interest and I were driving to the retreat, she called, screaming at the top of her lungs for me to come back. Shaking, I hung up the phone. My first thought was "Don't bring that into the meditation."

"Om kang kani kang kani..."

We are chanting for the victims of the Tsunami that hit Indonesia, just weeks before my affair was uncovered and devastated my life. I pray that as we are helping those souls cross over, it will help me cross over too, from this moment to a calmer, clearer one.

"rotzani rotzani"

My old life - 13 years together, a home, a business, 2 dogs, a successful bout with my partner's cancer. According to her, it is my fault. My family and friends agree. There I go again, screwing everything up. My new life is impossible to imagine. I am terrified of losing everything yet am driven by a force that leaves me with no choices.

"tro tra ni tro tra ni"

During the afternoon break, I have a one-on-one with the Lama. I share what I'm going through with her and she is quiet. She knows the other woman, a long-time student of hers. Give me some insights, I beg, what do I do now? "Focus on the words," she reminds me, "repeat them with your whole heart."

"tra sa ni tra sa ni"

The entire meditation and most of the instructions are in Tibetan. I feel awkward, unfamiliar with the protocols and rituals so I keep my eyes open and follow as best I can. I have no idea what I'm doing but I do it anyway, holding onto my faith that I'm getting something out of it, that the world will benefit from this act of making the sounds, doing the movements. When the discomfort from sitting becomes unbearable, I focus on the smell of the incense, which is good, and fill myself with its fragrance.

"prati hana prati hana"

At the end of the first day, I decide to drive back and face my partner and I am terrified. As I walk through the door to our home, I see her sitting on the couch. She is more hurt than I have ever seen her. I feel helpless. For the entire night, we go round and round, screaming then crying. She throws things, our things. Why? How? I try to explain that I was dying in my life. "I want to clean it up, make it better," I tell her. But I can't tell her that something has already been initiated. Not the affair but something inside of me that cannot be undone.

The next morning, after fighting all night, I drive back to the retreat. It's been almost 48 hours since I've slept but as soon as I begin chanting the mantra, I slide into a place of calmness, like being in the center of a hurricane. Although big chunks of my life have been uprooted and are crashing around me, I am okay. The mantra repeats in me over and over and over again and I dissolve into pure sound and join the others in one powerful wave.

"sarwa karma param para nime sarwa nantza soho"

After the retreat, my partner tells me she wants to see a Shaman as a last ditch effort to save our relationship. His name is Star Blanket. I don't know what a Shaman 'does' but I think "At least then I could then say I have tried every last thing, including a Shaman, before knowing that the relationship is over".

"How long have you been a Seeker?" Star Blanket asks me in our first session. I am not quite sure what he is asking so in a nonchalant way I say, "I don't know, maybe a month or two." He smiles and answers back, "How about your entire life?" It strikes me as an odd question and an even stranger answer! As I sit there and think further, I know he is right, yet I begin wondering, "Who is this guy and what does he think he knows about me?"

I am unaware that I am about to embark on a life journey of the soul and that this man holds the key. I have no idea where to start, what to do, or where to go. I just tell him I want to make another appointment, by myself.

A few months later, I am standing at the door of a house that is now 100% mine. It is completely empty. Feeling guilty about my affair, I have given my ex-partner all our furniture. Not wanting to lose my home, I cashed out all my stocks and savings to buy her out of her half of the house so I am now broke. But I refuse to give up the dogs. So here we are, Beasley, Zuni and me, in an empty shell of a house, watching her drive away and taking my old life with her.

Chapter 1 – Seed

"Think for the Self"

Star Blanket:

The circle is everywhere.

My energy field is a circle with the sun, moon, planets and stars.

The circle allows many viewing points that have multiple realities.

As I grow and learn from this circle of life, I am always a student.

As nature evolves, so does my circle of knowledge.

The foundation of the circle is critical to learn for energy moves and breathes the creative force within it.

Learn to think for the self by being in your own circle.

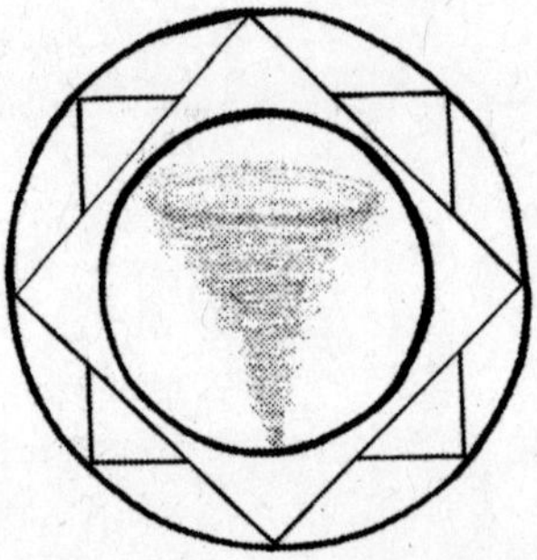

Dream Weaver:

My thoughts are racing around and around, circling my head as I prepare for my first Sunlight Dance, to journey deep into the heart of my true purpose. I know it's not in the high-tech industry where I've spent the last 20 years. Brushing my teeth takes on a note of solemnity as I imagine that I am cleansing myself to be inside the sacred space of the Medicine Wheel. I am excited and nervous and a little bit out of it, too. It takes me 20 minutes to find my car keys and when I do, they are right on the counter by the door. I grab them and rush out, not wanting to be late.

For the past 6 months, I've been feeling like I've been running to catch up on learning what I was never taught in college or work or life, following the trail of a shaman whom I met by chance, although I can hear him chuckling at the thought. "There are no chances", he has said many times. His name is Star Blanket and most times it doesn't feel like I've chosen to study with him as much as the choice was made for me. He has been teaching me the shamanic ways. I was called Sue and I would have been the last person you'd expect to be studying shamanism. Life has become very surprising.

My time is filled with lessons in energy, Medicine Wheels, and the connections between all things. Today, I will experience this knowledge in action in Nature for the first time. I can't wait.

There are 10 of us about to embark on this journey on this sunny, fall day. We are being led by Standing Flame, a bear of a man with bright blue eyes like the Colorado sky. This is his first time leading a journey and he is backed up by Star Blanket.

Everyone is from the healing professions except me. I try to ignore my insecurity from being the only one who's spent the past 20 years working with computers instead of people. "Why am I always the oddball in the group?" I wonder. Star Blanket, the Elder, invokes, "Grandfather, Grandmother we come to you in a good way, in the old way again. We ask you to hold us in good space while these Seekers quest their answers for life. We do not intend any hardship to any living thing. We all align with the divine plan of Truth for our evolution. Ah ho." We start walking in different directions, following our own callings.

The weight of my backpack feels comforting and grounding. I feel like a turtle with its protection and home on its back. I have prepared well, I think. Inside is my lodge notebook that includes the questions I will answer during this Ceremony, a pad, pen, tobacco for doing offering, sage and book of matches, a compass, various mixtures of medicine herbs that are used for sealing my circle during Ceremony, a rain jacket (because you never know when the weather will change in Colorado), and a pocket knife because you never know when you need a pocket knife when you're in the woods. All I need is the spot where I will set up my circle. Sounds easy and I imagine it will unfold as planned.

I begin walking, and walking, and walking. I go about 2 ½ miles into the forest, up a hill, down a hill, into a valley, and up another hill. An hour passes without me realizing it. Although I feel the need to be alone, I hadn't intended to go so far into the woods. This is when I realize my intentions are not guiding me now. I See that I have lost track of what I am doing and I haven't been paying attention to the landmarks around me, or my compass.

A clearing emerges that looks right and I begin setting up my Circle. I gather 8 stones and start placing them in each of the 8 directions, starting in the South and continuing around the wheel clockwise. With each stone, I remind myself of the power of that direction: S – willingness, SW – forgiveness, W – change, NW – faith, N – clarity, NE – love, E – unity, and SE – respect.

I call in my Ancestors and Spirits. They will help me learn what I need to learn. I'm hoping for some insights into how to find my way out of both a relationship and a career in which I've lost myself.

"I ask my spirit guides and ancestors to join me in this circle to help bring the lessons to me that I'm supposed to be learning in this Ceremony and do it with beauty, ease and grace." I call out to the Spirit of the trees, air, and sky and the Great Spirit.

Once I step inside the Circle, it's like being in a pressure cooker. Star Blanket has told me that I will be squeezed until whatever I need to look at comes up to the surface of my awareness. This way, it can be released. I know enough to know that it may have nothing to do with what is on my mind. I try to stay open but secretly, I'm hoping for a life-changing experience, something that will clarify all the confusion in my life.

My Circle is sealed. I am inside of it and ready to go through the questions and provide my answers. There are 9 questions, one for each of the eight directions plus the center, all relating to purpose like what is it, what's stopping me, what resources do I need to fulfill it? I start writing.

It takes longer than I anticipated and as I am writing, the weather starts to change. This is not unusual in Colorado. The weather can change at the drop of a hat. Unfortunately I don't have a hat with me. The wind picks up. It turns cold. Snow squalls roll in, surprising for this time of year. I am aggravated for not bringing more clothes. I will just tough it out. After all, it will only be a couple of hours.

It takes me hours to finish answering the questions but I am satisfied that I have completed the work I have come into the woods to do. I say to myself, "Well that wasn't so hard, it just took longer then I expected." As I am taking my Circle down, it begins to snow. Not just squall, but snow. Within 10 minutes, the ground is covered.

Directions are not my forté. Right and left have always been foreign concepts while driving or hiking. Usually, I rely on asking someone the correct way to go. This is the very first time I am so far in the forest off trail and will have to use my compass to guide me back to where I started. Star Blanket is supposed to be tracking us, meaning he's got a psychic connection to me and everyone on this journey, but I am not confident that he really can. My journey seems to be just beginning.

Everything starts looking the same. White. I am certain I am going the right way, only I have no idea how far away camp is. I am unaware that on the way in I had actually changed directions. Not knowing what else to do, I walk and walk and walk for about an hour. Fear sets in. People die all the time lost in the wilderness in Colorado. I am running low on water, have only one power bar for food, and a rain jacket for warmth. I am getting angry with myself for being so unprepared. I keep walking, just forging ahead, my mind racing trying to figure out what to do.

Fear turns into panic. Am I walking in the right direction? How far am I from camp? Am I going to end up spending the night out in the snow in the wilderness? There are bears and mountain lions around here. Then it happens. I hear the beat of a drum. Relief fills me. I am walking in the complete opposite direction and the drum turns me around. I start following the sound.

Then, the drumming stops. Panic returns! I think of the people 100 feet away from camp who end up freezing to death in a snowstorm because they can't see the campsite. I climb through a bog to keep my direction and find a dried-up deer leg bone. I pick it up as a medicine gift and start banging it on the side of my leg and singing to myself. The rhythm soothes me. Receiving this "gift" reminds me of the teaching that Spirit is always around me, watching me, talking to me. I give up trying to "figure it out", humbled by my own ignorance, and focus on keeping my eyes and ears open, on listening with my entire being.

Another sound comes through the woods. This time it is a truck roaring in the distance. Spirit speaks with many voices. I can't tell how far away it is because sometimes sound travels far in the mountains but if I follow the sound of the truck, it will eventually bring me to the highway. I have no idea where I might come out, but if I have to I can hitchhike back to camp.

Climbing another hill and then down the other side, I finally reach the road after crawling under a barbed wire fence. If you have never tried to crawl under barbed wire, I don't recommend it. It is starting to get dark. Once I get to the highway, I am not sure which way to go so I do something unusual, I follow my gut. It turns out to be the right way. Within half –a-mile, I see the sign for the dirt road up to camp. I am flooded with relief.

Hours have passed since I left camp. This Sunlight Dance has turned into a Sun Down Dance for me. There are 3-4 inches of snow already on the ground. I am nearly three miles from where I need to be. At this point I am determined to make it back on my own. I am singing and banging my deer bone on my leg, freezing cold, covered in snow, and in a ripped jacket from the barbed wire.

Triumph mixes with embarrassment as I walk into camp from the complete opposite direction from where I started. Standing Flame, who has been drumming for me, is visibly relieved that he didn't lose someone on his first Sunlight Dance. Star Blanket is there too, waiting beside a fire they have built to keep warm. Star Blanket simply says, 'Welcome back'. It is the very first time in my life that I found my own way.

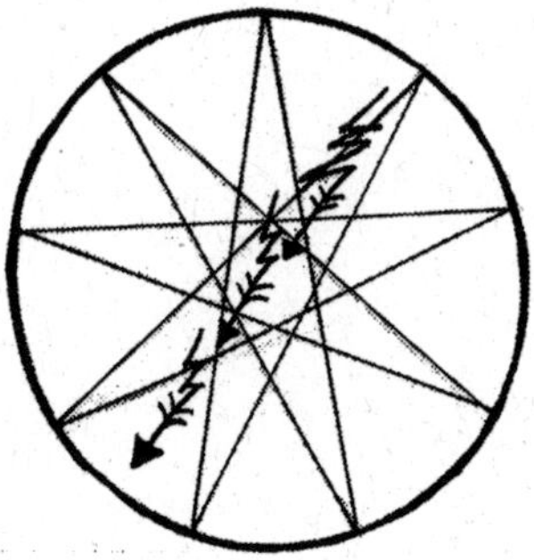

Later, I learn that nobody else walked more than a couple of hundred yards from camp. In the future I will figure out that everything I need to learn is inside of me, that I can set up my Circle right where I'm standing and it will be perfect. But that's a few years away.

Star Blanket:
Everyone has a link to The Everything and everyone has a navigation system. Although buried in illusions, distortions and diversion, the First Agenda of Renewal Trails is to remember this link, sort out the distortions, and train. The training for this level continues until an acceptable percentage of accuracy of thinking for the self occurs. The alternative is the faceless spirit of Coyote finding ways to play with your ego. This link to The Everything

is never severed. Each Seeker must surrender to the energy forces of The Everything. This is where you will learn again.

Chapter 2 – Union

"Practice Co-Creation"

Star Blanket:

As a seed unites into the ground, the process of creating a relationship begins. The elemental resources Earth, Air, Fire, and Water begin their magic of opening the relationship and co-creating. Life as humans is the same. When beginning a project, friendship, or relocation, seeds have to be planted and the relationship given energetic support in order to flourish. As in the plant world, a seed does not grow on its own. The Mother Earth is sacred as is her essence to allow all her children to create with her. A tree grows in balance by giving and receiving. This is being part of the whole and individual with purpose.

Dream Weaver:

"Trust me," Star Blankets eyes say. We are sitting in the Circle and it is jammed, meaning that energy is not flowing freely. There's something that people aren't being open about due to risk exposure. Star Blanket is leading and turns to me, wanting me to share a story I had told him the day before. I don't want to. It is too personal. I know all these people and see them on a daily basis and he is asking me to risk sharing a story that I have told maybe 2 people in my entire life. Is he using me to get this Circle moving?

With a deep breath, I begin anyway, trusting him. "I was 17 years old, untouched and curious. I was about to leave for college which made me brave, thinking I wouldn't have to deal with the consequences of fooling around so we did. He was one of my closest friends. We got naked. I got pregnant. But we did not actually have sex. It was incomprehensible to him. I decided to have an abortion because I had a life to live that didn't include becoming a mother. He told me he would go with me but when the day came, he backed out, saying it was too hard for him. I was livid."

Although I was unsure, Star Blanket was right. My words are like a key and when I speak them, the Circle opens. People start popping, telling stories of their abortions and botched attempts at connecting sexually. It isn't until I release the story to the Circle, that I notice how much energy I'd spent hiding it. We are all able to look into each other's eyes now. There will be no secrets.

About a year has passed since that Circle and in that time I have become an apprentice to the Bundle of Knowledge that Star Blanket carries. During one of our regular phone calls, he says that it is time for me to receive my Spirit Name. Am I ready?

Nicknames dot my life, each one like a dog collar that's a little too tight; something other people use to put me in a box, reflecting only a slice of me. But taking a Spirit Name is different. In the shamanic tradition, it is a path back to one's original purity and puts us in relationship with the moment we were born. It is our true name. Instead of representing my place in my blood family, it will activate my place in the cosmic family.

The Spirit Name carries medicine that you grow into meaning it represents who you will become. Every time it is used, it will remind me of my true essence and my relationship to nature. The name Sue Spielman carried a distorted relationship to the natural world. The taking of a name, will open up my toughest and most challenging lessons in order to embody my highest possibilities whether I want to or not. Star Blanket asks me to take this into consideration before deciding if I really want to take a name. Without any hesitation, I say yes.

My Taking of a Spirit Name Ceremony is choreographed by Star Blanket. There is a full Mesa, which is like an altar in the center of a huge room. Standing Flame assists by leading songs on the big Medicine Drum as we all sing along. When Star Blanket begins, memories of not belonging flood every part of my body, memories

of being different than the Spielman clan, of feeling different among my colleagues and of being gay in a very straight, male world. Now here I am, sitting in the center of Circle, with everyone singing for me. I feel like I'm in a womb and about to step through a Sacred Hoop and be reborn. Star Blanket retrieved the vision of my birth. The name is in the vision. The name will not come for a few more days but I am beginning a kind of labor to birth it.

For the next few days, I prepare a Sweat Lodge for our community. After assisting in building the Fire, I lie down on the grass and take a break. I am looking at the sky and close my eyes, thinking about my naming Ceremony. Something has changed. I can feel it in my body. I run up to Star Blanket and Standing Flame and announce that I have my name. As I speak the name out loud, it doesn't feel right. Star Blanket smiles, and says, 'Keep Dreaming with it'. So I go back to the grass and lay down. A few more minutes pass. Ah ha! Now I really have it. I march back to them. Again…as I say it out loud, something doesn't fit. I am beginning to doubt myself so I am really hoping I have it this time. "Nope", Star Blanket says.

Resigned to the fact that I am going to be eternally nameless, I go back to tending to the Fire. After another hour or so, I lay back down on the grass. With my eyes closed, the whole name appears, "Dream Weaver of the Crane's Flight". I sit straight up, and say out loud "Crane's? I don't have anything to do with cranes!" I have a whole conversation with myself about having no connection with birds and that a crane cannot be part of my name. My name should be something like lion or jaguar. I must be making this crane thing up so I slowly lower myself back down to the grass. The name keeps repeating in my head, over and over. I open my eyes and am staring at the sky, hopeless. At that moment, two cranes fly directly over my head. I have never seen one before in Colorado, or anywhere else for that matter. This time, I walk over to Star Blanket and instead of thinking I have my name, I know it. "Dream Weaver of the Crane's Flight," I say. Star Blanket smiles and says, "Ah-ho".

I have come to learn that certain Ceremonies are passages from one reality into another. This is called the Sacred Hoop. The taking of a name is one of those passages. I am about to begin a new life. This time, though, it will be one that I create myself.

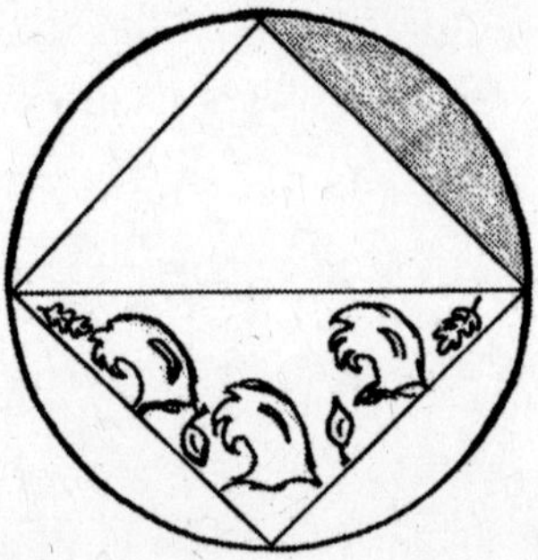

Star Blanket:

Water is the main element in the human, plant and animal bodies and is the carrier of encoded memory from both RNA and DNA strands. When a vision is experienced in a sacred way to recall ones essence at the time of birth, an animal or plant can symbolically call upon the waters codes. This is often the case with Right of Passage ceremonies like the "Taking of Spirit Name".

Imprinting is a process of repeating, until the experience is recorded in a body memory. This is done by including the audio, visual, taste, smell and touch senses. This process is done everyday whether we are aware of it or not, whether an athlete, musician, parent or office worker, a habitual pattern of repetition will record an imprint. An example of this in ceremonial healing is when a Seeker is experiencing fantasies or nightmares. Often I will smell popcorn and melted butter. Because of the smells, that tells me they have picked up a stimulus from going to the movies. If we can trace the trail of imprinting the core will reveal a fear that has been masked over and stimulated by a trip to the movies.

The essence of imprinting can be limiting or expansive depending upon the individual's history. The fluidity of many drinks that contain tastes and smells can also be a stimulus that awakens memory. Animals are great teachers when observed smelling their food and water. They have a link to recorded imprints that determine their decision to drink and eat. Humans have this same ability. For the awakened Seeker, the decision to engage in an experience will eventually be based on the choice of revealing past imprinting or to create new ones.

Chapter 3 – Egg

"All Battles Are With the Self "

Cahokia, Illinois, USA 2006 A.D.

Dream Weaver:

Star Blanket, Thunderbird Woman and I are packing the Toyota. I am assisting for the first time as Dream Weaver. It is time for a medicine journey. Actually, any journey is a medicine journey; it is just taking me time to realize it. Whether it is a land of canyons or the grocery store, each journey becomes a medicine journey in its own way. This means there is always something to learn from it. More and more events are happening in my life that makes it seem as if each is separate from the others; my work here, my relationships there, my spiritual stuff in that box. I am in the process of learning how to unwind my way of existing up to this point in my life, unwinding my thinking that there is actually a separation in these areas. In fact, each is related and if I am listening carefully they are all giving me pieces of the puzzle, the puzzle being myself.

Star Blanket and I are doing many healing sessions together to continue this unwinding. It seems like these take place on a daily basis. We do sessions on clearing out my Genetic Rivers. This takes place over a series of months. Genetic Rivers are meridians in the body. I have come to learn they are called by many names in other traditions. We are removing imprints that I might have been carrying forward for years, even many lifetimes. I am realizing more and more that this path I am embarking on is much greater than I had expected. These sessions reveal layer after layer of illusions. Slowly things I believed in no longer look so appealing. These include my career, some of my friends, my relationships. I begin to wonder when Star Blanket and I will reach the end of the series. Like a movie, I want an end. I continue doing all that I need to keep opening up the memories in my body. I am looking at every aspect, my friends, my family, my career, my hobbies, my relationships and evaluating what is really the core of each of them. It is an eye opening experience to have aspects revealed right before my eyes and this unfolding jumps to another level whenever I go on another journey.

I had been to this small town in southern Illinois on two other occasions. Both occasions had been for training lodges that Star Blanket was teaching. Each experience taught me more and more about how the path of the medicine effects and affects all different folks. There are all age ranges from 6 to 60. Each person brings his own stories and motivations for being there. I bring mine. My thoughts are that I am being put in an assistant role. Not only will I be a participant but I will also be helping others during the lodge and basically doing what Star Blanket requests. I've been in a leadership role in the corporate world for many years, managing people, projects, budgets. Even with those skills under my belt, this is a whole different thing. I am starting everything over in terms of how I look at events to determine what is necessary; the unwinding of myself is continuing.

Star Blanket, Thunderbird Woman and I set out for Illinois from Colorado late in the afternoon of a Wednesday. Thunderbird Woman is another student whom I had known from other events we've experienced, but this is our first medicine journey together. We are friendly, but don't actually know each other very well. The friendship is more on a casual level and a respect for each other knowing that we are both attempting to walk this path. This particular medicine journey will bring our friendship to a new level. We are setting out for the 17-hour drive in Star Blanket's grey Toyota Sequoia, also known as the Rhino. We will make it as far as we can on Wednesday into the night, stop somewhere, and then start again in the morning. We need to reach southern Illinois by Thursday night since the training lodge is starting on Friday and we will need some prep and organization time.

We load our stuff into the truck along with medicine tools such as various feathers, rattles, and other items that will be used as necessary throughout the lodge. There are also several blankets for the Sweat Lodge. Many of the items will be placed on a Mesa like alter that would be present throughout the lodge. Two large medicine blankets are placed in the center of the room where we gather. The medicine items are placed on the medicine blankets to represent a Mesa. The symbols of all of the Mesa items carry the knowledge being presented from the Renewal Trails Bundle. This is the Bundle that Star Blanket is Keeper of.

The truck is fully packed and we're ready to go. I am tuning in to the importance of paying attention to everything that is going on. That "Everything is related" concept that Star Blanket has been telling me about is starting to sink in. Being in Ceremony brings it to the consciousness even more. I will find out en route how all the items fit.

This is the very first medicine journey where I am actually traveling with Star Blanket. While I'd been on other journeys before, I am always caravanning in another car. Star Blanket would be the lead bird, and we'd be following. This trip is different. We will all be in the car together, and that by itself is a teaching. I am experiencing seeing how everything going on between us in the car, the conversations, the emotions being brought to the surface, will be presenting itself in the lodge over the next couple of days. We head down the long road, making our way out of Colorado heading east towards Kansas. It doesn't take long for the magic and mystery to start unfolding.

A conversation starts about the Divine Feminine. Star Blanket starts teaching. We are all part of the dream taking place and for the last 8 hours we have been walking through a portal opening. The trail is what is called The Tribal Tree. We are in what seems like a bubble. Star Blanket continues, "The Tribal Tree Trails are the meridian paths that humans retrace their personal history

through many lifetimes to reclaim the feminine principle of the authentic self. Some traditions call this essence within these meridians the Christ, Buddha and a host of other titles. There is a map in the body that also acts like a measure of where the Seeker is at on the trail. Every human experience passes through individualized meridians." The Rhino goes quiet as Star Blanket finishes. It is almost like a blueprint is put in front of us to tell where the evolution of our soul is. It is late into the night when we agree that we should probably stop and rest for the night. We are exhausted and electrified.

Rising the next morning, the journey continues through the day and into Thursday night. We are giddy and laugh a lot as we pull into the training lodge. We enter the little town in Southern Illinois around 11 O'clock that night and get a room at the local hotel. This will be a big weekend. Star Blanket tells Thunderbird Woman and me to get some rest. We'd need to be on full power in the morning.

Thunderbird Woman and I are forming a bond. We are realizing that we are in the middle of experiencing something very different than either one of us had experienced before. We are assisting Star Blanket with this teaching. Realizing this, we both know instinctively that we will help each other out. We are working together as a team and it is pretty clear that our Tribal paths had crossed before. There is fluidity about the way we move. We start calling ourselves the 'Yoni Sisters'. We head to our rooms because we know Star Blanket is right. We'd need to be rested in the morning. The Tribal Tree Trail of the Renewal Trails Bundle wants birthing.

Morning comes and we are warmly greeted as we arrive. The opening Talking Stick reveals the intensity of our drive. We have the laughs, tears, learning, sharing, and intimacy that all lodges have. Experiencing the Circle is something that is hard to forget. Energy moves in the Circle and will keep flowing around and around in the Circle until it reaches a point of release. And that will be the person that speaks for the Circle. While on first glance it might appear that it's that person's issue, it will be revealed that somewhere each and every person in the Circle carries fragments of the expression. It is slightly different but ultimately it will be a similar lesson. We call this a mirror of reflection. I continue to learn faith in the Circle and my key to the faith is to get my mind out of the way. Old Coyote is a good teacher in this way.

The next day, Star Blanket introduces the quest of researching the healing powers of Awakened Water, The Tribal Tree Trail, and the vision for a community living in a harmonious way with nature. All goes smoothly and yet I continue to sense a progressive anxiety. The training lodge and the closing Sweat Lodge are full of challenges and reflections.

Saturday evening is full of excitement as the group separates by gender to experience a shift out of the present point on the Tribal Tree blueprint. This exercise is to move out of the present perceptions into an observing point of view. The evening goes well with few exceptions. The lingering sensation of resistance seems to be gone as we close for the night. I awake Sunday morning to a slight headache. I know something has gotten activated the night before. I decide to let the day reveal the imprints that I need to face.

We arrive shortly before the group and start setting up the room. Thunderbird Woman and I smudge the space and straighten up the Mesa. Chaos follows! Star Blanket has explained the "Return" many times but I never had to assist in directing the movement. It seems to me that many participants are trying to control the design of the day. I approach Star Blanket and ask what we should do. Star Blanket responds, "The human ego is fragile when confronted with more realities. This is acceptable. We must stay focused on making medicine the best we can. The answers are inside you. The outside world, whether you are teaching or walking around your home will match the conflicts inside. The teachings of water, body star maps and the magic of these ways often demand a change in lifestyle standards. If the teachers can't or won't change then the chaos will be doubled when presenting. This is the resistance we are finding today. They are good people. Treat them like you would yourself."

There is something in the way that Star Blanket says, "If the teachers can't or won't change then the chaos will be doubled" that I know I need to look inside and I need to do it fast. I am in a teacher role here. I need to do whatever I can to be in good medicine. In other words, I need to face my own demons and see the mirrors in my own life so that others in the lodge could be as open as possible to see theirs. If I hold onto my own issues, everyone else will hold onto theirs as well. I need a few moments to understand what Star Blanket has just spoken and go outside for a short walk around the land. I am praying to the Spirits to illuminate for me what I need to see so that I will not be blocking the energy for the group. As I walk around, I start replaying events in my head that have happened over the course of the last few months to see what the relationship is to what is happening in the moment now. One event stands out.

About a month before, I was in New York City for a meeting as a technology consultant with a client. I was staying at the Waldorf Astoria, a well-known landmark in Manhattan. Not to mention a very expensive hotel, even by Manhattan standards. As soon as I arrived and checked in I started to not feel so well. I had a three-day meeting taking place and knew that it would not be a good time to be sick. I came back to my room after the first day, and was sick as a dog. I had a massive migraine, I started throwing up and cold sweats were coming in waves. My body was actually shaking. I felt my whole body caving in, like there was a vice being tightened around me. I was on my hands and knees in the floor of this room in this fancy hotel and reached for my phone to call Star Blanket. I knew I needed some help. I also knew that there was something energetic going on that was making me so sick; it wasn't that I had caught a bug as it might be appearing.

Star Blanket answered his phone and I asked for help. I told him what was going on and for the next two hours we proceeded to do healings. As it turned out, my body was being used as a vehicle for many spirits, or ghosts, from the prohibition timeframe to help them cross over into a different dimension. They were attaching to my body because they knew I would be able to help them. I was accepting the responsibility of my medicine and helping them even though I knew I also had a responsibility for the reality I was in for my clients. It was also part of my Karma for the times when I was irresponsible in those ways and using my skills to exploit people. I was being pulled into two different worlds and had to not transfer the responsibility of either. It was past midnight when Star Blanket and I had finished. I felt the last of the Spirits leaving my body and was finally able to rest. It was like a giant weight was lifted off of me. I slept the remainder of the night and went to work the next morning for my clients.

The whole scenario from the night in New York is playing through my head as I walk around outside the Lodge. That experience taught me of the conflict that comes when I don't want to give something up in my lifestyle and also when I have to face something that might not be so pretty about myself. I am staying at a fancy NY hotel and felt that I didn't have any repercussions in my life for doing so. I needed to be able to stay open to what I had a responsibility for in the medicine that I am opening up in my body, even in this environment.

Looking at this experience in the observer role is helping it all to start coming into focus. I need to keep true to modeling the teachings I am learning, actually living them, if I am going to be teaching them. I see the mirror in my own life and walk back into the lodge hoping that I will be able to help others open that mirror up. I understand the words Star Blanket spoke to Thunderbird Woman and me. Understanding this allows me to walk calmly around the Sacred Fire for the Sweat Lodge that evening. I go back to the Sacred Fire and it is much calmer when I am working from my center. The Sweat continues that night and I help bring the lodge to the end. We close in a good way, pack up and go to our motel. An incomplete sensation continues as we eat dinner and talk about the strengths and weaknesses that we faced.

I go to bed thinking that there was no break-through during the weekend. Something was missing. I keep thinking that usually in other gatherings that I've attended there was an intensity that would build that included some kind of peak break-through being reached. Then there would always be calm after the storm that would complete the gathering. This one didn't have that. This journey must not be done.

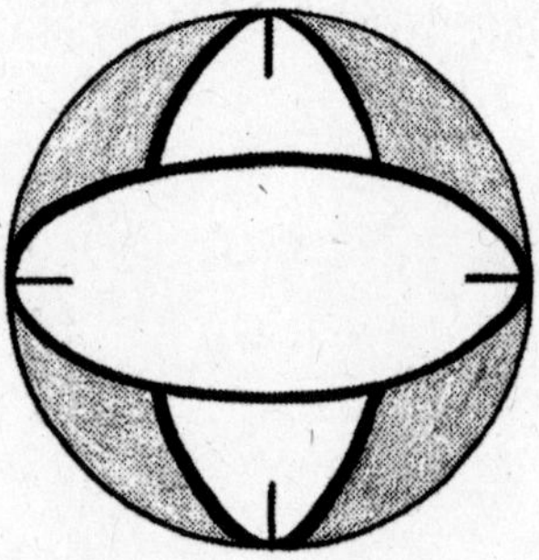

The next morning, I sit up fast as the cell phone blasts the morning dream out of my body. It is Star Blanket. "We're going to Cahokia. We are not done with the peak of this journey yet. Meet in the lobby." I hang up and relay the message to a sleepy Thunderbird Woman. I know from past experiences that Star Blanket means get moving at a steady pace. We are in the lobby in an hour. It seems like it will be an interesting stop on the ride home, even though it is in a different direction of the way home, but Spirit is guiding us and we are following the lead.

I am trying to learn the difference between what I would consider my logical mind working and being guided by Spirit. Logically we would head South West back to Denver however having the incomplete sensation that I had last night, it makes sense that we're heading South! Coyote must have been busy last night.

The Cahokia web site reads:

The remains of the most sophisticated prehistoric native civilization north of Mexico are preserved at Cahokia Mounds State Historic Site. Within the 2,200-acre tract, located a few miles west of Collinsville, Illinois, lie the archaeological remnants of the central section of the ancient settlement that is today known as Cahokia.

Cahokia Mounds has been recognized as a U. S. National Historic Landmark, and the United Nations Educational,

Scientific, and Cultural Organization (UNESCO), in 1982, designated Cahokia Mounds a World Heritage Site for its importance to our understanding of the prehistory of North America. Cahokia Mounds is managed by the Illinois Historic Preservation Agency.

According to archaeological finds, the city of Cahokia was inhabited from about A.D. 700 to 1400. At its peak, from A.D. 1050 to 1200, the city covered nearly six square miles and possibly 10-20,000 people lived here. Over 120 mounds were built through time, and most mounds were enlarged several times. Houses were arranged in rows and around open plazas, and the main agricultural fields lay outside the city. The site is named for a subtribe of the Illiniwek (or Illinois tribe, a loose confederacy of related peoples) - the Cahokia - who moved into this area in the 1600s and lived nearby when the French arrived about 1699. Sometime in the mid-1800s, local historians suggested the site be called "Cahokia" to honor these later arrivals. Archaeological investigations and scientific tests, mostly since the 1920s and especially since the 1960s, have provided what is known of the once-thriving community.

The fate of the prehistoric Cahokians and their city is unknown, but the decline seems to have been gradual, beginning in the 1200s and the site had been abandoned by A.D. 1400. Exactly where the people went or what tribes they became is yet to be determined. Depletion of resources probably contributed to the city's decline. A climate change after A.D. 1200 may have affected crop production and the plant and animal resources needed to sustain a large population. War, disease, social unrest, and declining political and economic power may have also taken their toll."

We arrive at the mounds and have them practically to ourselves. Something magical is happening. We are entering a timeline that is waking something up in all of us, and also bringing something together between us.

The three of us sit in a theater in the welcome center that is showing a short film on the history of the Cahokia mounds. We are the only three in the theater that probably sits 100 people. As we watch the film, it is as if we are watching ourselves from that lifetime. We are actually there experiencing the familiar setting that is being shown on the screen. It is after this film that we do a short walk around the welcome center. We stop in our tracks as we walk up to an exhibit that shows the daily life of the people. There is a man and a woman and a dog in it. We all look at each other realizing that the man is Standing Flame, the woman is Thunderbird Woman, and the dog is an exact replica of Dinga, Standing Flames' dog. It is clear there is something else going on here besides a museum visit. It is becoming clearer and clearer to me that nothing is an accident and everything is related. My journey with Star Blanket is taking another turn and going to another level.

Outside the welcome center we climb to the top of the highest mound. It is said that this is ceremonial ground. Looking out from the top of the mound I walk a bit on my own. I am gazing out across the land. There is a giant structure of poles. I know it has to be some type of astrological time keeping mechanism that was used by the people who were living there. I start having memories of it. I remember seeing Star Blanket standing about 100 ft from me. He is looking at Thunderbird Woman and me. We are being reunited on a different level. It is intoxicating.

We spend about 45 minutes at the top of the mound. We are realizing that we are receiving a download of information, for how a complete community functioned while being in alignment with the land. We are also being told what happens when you are not in alignment with the land. Cahokia is a global mirror about the use of resources. Current global resources are also being depleted at an alarming rate. Our own presentation about living with nature will take some major lifestyle changes for us. It is being drilled into us that All Battles are with the Self, no matter what size community you are in. Coyote tricked us into our own introspection. I can hear the howling laugh in the wind.

I think of how to proceed with our project of the community that includes the water research. I don't know what the reflection of Cahokia means, I just know that something is happening and to just to be with it. The community at Cahokia seemed to perish because it was out of alignment due to the way the resources were used. Nature's ways were out of balance. Star Blanket had spoke many times about the Natural Law called "Conservation and Efficient use of Energy Resources". The law was somehow misused by the inhabitants of Cahokia. My thoughts race as we climb the steps of the highest mound. Perhaps this is the mound of the ruling power. The mistake was probably that the ruling power became a person instead of letting the ruling power be the Nature's Ways. In some cosmic way, it all makes sense. However it is still a stretch for me to actually understand it. Eventually we make our way down from the top of the main mound. We are definitely in an altered state. That's when the laughter begins.

I wonder how to explain what it feels like when I enter these altered states. The closest thing I can compare it to is when you are laughing so hard that your stomach hurts and then you start laughing some more. And really, you have no idea what you're laughing at. It could resemble being drunk, only we aren't. Although other people think we were. It is already late in the afternoon and we know we have to get on the road to start back to Colorado. The whole day had been spent with the Cahokia experience, only we didn't realize it had passed the day. It is as if we are in some type of vortex. All three of us think it best that we go get some coffee before starting on the long drive home. That is the beginning of one of the longest laughing fits I think I've ever had in my life. And the funniest part is that it was over a muffin in a coffee shop.

Thunderbird Woman and I are waiting to pay for coffee. Star

Blanket is in the bathroom at the time. Thunderbird woman and I look at the counter with the muffin on it and we both start laughing so hard that we end up on the floor. Both of us are on the floor practically crying from laughing, we can't even speak we are laughing so hard, and Star Blanket walks out of the bathroom. He looks at us and starts laughing too. So here we are, all three of us laughing. And we can't stop. The poor woman waiting to take our money for the coffee has no idea what is happening and can only assume that we are totally drunk. We are assuring her that we aren't and keep laughing on the floor. What a spectacle we must have been. But it is all a result of what is being awakened in our body. Being on the mounds, we opened up to something from a time long ago. The Renewal Trails Bundle is coming alive in us. Coyote will reveal the answer along the way.

It is a long 17-hour ride home. We talk a lot, going through what happened over the course of the last 5 days. There is a lot to recapitulate, or assimilate, into our bodies. Many times, even when a lodge has completed in the physical, there are still energy movements going on that will be a result of things that had happened during the lodge. This journey is no exception. When the laughing sobers and a quiet enters the Rhino, Star Blanket speaks, "Okay ladies we have a few hours drive tonight before resting. What did we learn?"

I know from past experience that when Star Blanket is asking what we had learned, it is time to reflect back on everything that happened and try and thread the beads together. Every event, every conversation, every emotion that anyone had would all be related through the thread of common experiences. I stare out the window for a while watching the billboards go by on the highway. There is a quiet in the car, but Star Blanket knows we are just being with the question he asked. I am processing and seeing what pieces stand out to me and what the mirrors are in my own life.

I start to speak out loud in response to Star Blanket's question.

"I've learned, once again, that everything is related. Getting to participate as an assistant in the lodge, riding in the Rhino and visiting Cahokia accelerated the mirrors. Whenever there was the chance of conflict, I went inside to face myself. If I didn't want to face it, I would either transfer my issue to the student or direct the energy in such as way as to discredit that personality. I am realizing I often transfer issues in my life. I am continually hitting walls of my denial, like when the headaches come on." The truck goes silent except for the wind howling across the kayak rack on top.

After sharing I go back to staring out the window for a while, letting it all sink in. I am entering a new solidified place with my relationship with Star Blanket. I think about running rocks for the Sweat Lodge, the Talking Stick Circles and Cahokia. I know there is something going on inside me that isn't at peace. My life is taking a whole new form. I am accepting the responsibility that All Battles are mine. Over the last months the migraine headaches have lessoned. I still keep the medication handy, but only use it occasionally. Something about accepting responsibility is changing my dependence on the medication.

Maybe it is ten minutes, maybe an hour. I'm not sure. Star Blanket's question lingers in the Rhino like a cloud that will only clear when the truth is spoken. Another pattern occurs to me. It was triggered by standing on top of the mound at Cahokia. I start speaking.

"Nature would always be the ultimate mirror. Humans have been so irresponsible with the use of resources during the course of history, and none more so than in the time we are currently living in. Yet I don't want to give up my lifestyle. Could I give up a shower each day or not taking plane trips when I want to? Nature thrives to be efficient and it will do whatever needs to be done to operate that way. I know the mirror is the efficient use of resources. Things are not as they appear." Other thoughts are popping into my head of the events that have happened. I continue speaking as we drive. “This training lodge is also a time of experiencing the water.” Star Blanket and I had done a blessing on the water before we left and had a number of gallons with us that we had loaded in the truck. I had been the Fire Chief for the first time. I did the design of the Sacred Fire and running the rocks with the other Fire Keepers. It was all done in a very specific and sacred design and choreography. The fire reflects exactly what everyone is experiencing and processing.

Star Blanket had poured the blessed water on hot rocks creating the steam inside the Sweat Lodge. It helped people move emotions that were rising to the surface from opening the Tribal Tree teaching. My thoughts continue without words. The Sweat Lodge is an efficient use of energy!

The thought bursts into my head like a freight trains whistle. Loudly I speak “Could our United States be heading for a similar fate as Cahokia?” The Rhino is silent. I continue, “Maybe the Earth?” Star Blanket responds by reminding me of a recent report released from the EPA. The report gave a gloomy outlook about the United States fresh water supply. The cloud in the Rhino clears, as we hear Coyote gently tapping on the window.

Chapter 4 – Sprout

"Truth Gives Movement"

Conifer, Colorado USA May 2006 A.D.

Star Blanket:

Now back at home in Conifer, Colorado and resuming daily chores and duties as Star Blanket, the trip to Illinois has worn off and all of the blankets and medicine items have been cleaned and stored away. I can feel the intensity from all the information integrating in my body after our trip to Cahokia and know that this night the sleeping dreams are going to be full.

A vision of the last year had returned in the night. My dreams seemed full after the trip through Cahokia. The vision begins with picturesque mountains. As the vision expands, I watch as water bubbles up out of Mother Earth, like clear milk nourishing all that gazes upon the beauty of its power and purpose. Several people are gathered, cheering like it is the end of a long wait. The water cascades down a stone lattice splashing over and through crystals, gems, sand, flowers, trees, sunlight, and soft winds. Like a river knowing its destination, it winds through a man-made greenhouse with an open skylight. The greenhouse is surrounded by a park with ponds, streams, plants, and animals, all providing songs echoing through the land. Soft music pleases the Spirits of the water, as fire-keepers of the healing arts make daily honoring. The whole area echoes a rhythm like the only priority is the enjoyment of life-giving moments. The sacred water flows through ceremonial mesas with nature's imprinting. Imprinting is the process by which we record memory. This imprinting carries the codes required to regenerate the sacred geometry.

I awaken to the sunlight coming in my window. In a flash I remember last night's dream. Grandmother Too Many Red Foxes had given me a teaching kind of-lecture. She said the wind had settled in our movement. It was time for some scouting. She said, "Research some areas around Sun Valley, Idaho. Coyote will be with you and remember Cahokia." I roll out of bed and wander to the coffee grinder. My growing financial stress takes my focus. The coffee grinder is at full speed when the focus collapses. Coffee grounds fly everywhere! I continue to grumble while cleaning up. I swear I could hear Grandmother and Coyote laughing. In stereo! "That is a scary feeling." I call Dream Weaver and we make a plan to leave for southern Idaho.

Our quest is to scout potential land, hot springs, kindred peers, and water rights that may be available for purchase in order to create the community in the vision. As we drive out of Colorado west towards Sun Valley, I am preparing to respond to Dream Weaver. She has asked about how all of our journeys are connected. The thoughts race by, of the training lodge, Cahokia, prophecies and Al Gore's recent book about Global Warming, called "An Inconvenient Truth". Dream Weaver pulls out a tape recorder and hangs a microphone over the rear view mirror. She is ready! I begin "A long time ago when my life was spared by the spirit world, I made a dedication to assist the animals, humans and Earth to cycle towards balance."

"Today I understand this purpose as the Medicine Ways of the Métis. In the last 10 years, many signs of Earth's resources being depleted are causing changes of climates, extinction of species and human migrations. If we peel back the layers of our recent adventures some common threads appear. The water supplies are drying up and yet humans use more. Global warming is real and yet measures are slow in reacting. A deep level of intimacy and honesty has been in all of our Circles and yet the resistance is strong." The truck goes quiet as we drift off pondering the thoughts. The echoes of Coyote's tricks seem to spread across the land.

We're on I-80, in the center of Wyoming. Our journey is taking us towards Salt Lake City, Utah and then up to southern Idaho into Twin Falls and the Saw Tooth mountain area. We are hoping to find Trinity Water bottlers, near Ketchum, Idaho. Their website says that one of the main attributes of their water is that the water carbon dates to 16,000 years old and it surfaces though 2.2 miles of crystal-lined faults. This type of water has a special link to the Divine Mother. Shamanic practices believe that crystals are the brains of Mother Earth. This is a quality that requires preservation. We want to explore the area and talk to some of the people involved with the water. Dream Weaver had made numerous phone calls and e-mails to water bottling companies in southern Idaho. No calls have been returned but we are hoping that once we arrive, something will open up.

Dream Weaver:

I ask Star Blanket, "How did the medicine men and women actually read the codes from the water and what has this to do with the current quest for water rights?" He answers, "Have you ever played with sticks in a stream after a rain?" I nod a yes and answer, "The stick will go wherever the water goes." Star Blanket responds, "Yes and where does the water go?" Before I can answer, Star Blanket continues, "To the source. We have sent out our intent and when we stay focused, that intent will bring us to the source of our quest."

Star Blanket continues, "There is a rising global need for fresh water. Population growth is out of control. Humans are using their sexual energy and powers to create everywhere. There is a lack of accountability for the use of these creative powers. Water is a closed system. There is no new water, only a flow cycling from the earth to the sky and back to the earth. Rain comes down, runs to holding areas, some evaporates and some goes into the Mother Earth. Water's movement is a cycle. Maybe the current melting of the ice caps is a result of the needs for fresh water." The restless warriors are securing rights to air, water, earth, and eventually fire. They know that folks will throw away electronics, quit driving cars and other extras, but elements like water?" Star Blanket pauses, letting this sink in. "The time to act is now."

He continues, "The spirit of Coyote is going global. There is a breaking down of current methods of regulating order. Order is regulated by the fourth dimension. The fourth dimension releases information from its mass like unplugging a drain. It comes in gobs or in trinkets. The information must be integrated slow and steady. This is the playground of Coyote. Humans often interpret the distorted information and images being released from the fourth dimension as being a spiritual transmission. Yet the fourth dimension is a compressed sea of thoughts all muddied together. Kind of like a garbage dump of unfinished experiences. The experiences must be finished before a new blueprint for Earth's evolution can be seeded into Earths minerals. The layer of the fourth dimension is unraveling, leaving in its wake the unfinished business of balancing the Earth's resources as a collective debt."

"Coyote will continue to challenge our technology and ingenuity until we balance our own lives. We are very skilled at converting energy from one form to another. This is our strength. The weakness can be understood through Coyote medicine. Humans trick themselves into diverting the responsibility to someone else. How many non-profit organizations does it take to pretend that we are 'doing good', while building million dollar homes out of vanishing oxygen-giving forests?"

After stopping for gas and coffee, I turn on the recorder. Star Blanket continues, "Water has been essential in many aspects of our ancestor's lives. The waterways provided travel, food, and trading, which assisted in communication. Medicine herbs, stories, songs and other goods were also exchanged by way of water travel. Health and quality of life largely depended upon clean water, as it does today. You have probably seen smoke signals, as a way of communicating in movies about Natives. Reading and sending coded messages was an art. Praying with and over water is an art form as well. The art is being lost to our scientific ways but Grandmother is saying it is time to bring these arts back in a scientific way. Research and magic will have to cooperate to achieve this."

The heaviness is thick as Star Blanket and I both quietly go into introspection of where we are out of balance with the earth, and in our personal lives. We soon stop for the night.

Star Blanket:

The next morning, we drive into Idaho and enter an area near Pine, Idaho. A beautiful reservoir greets us as we look for hot springs and the Trinity Water Company. Scouting is one of the Shamanic traits that we practice for times like this. For an hour or more we drive through the area. We finally find the plant and it is abandoned and locked up. There are no bankruptcy signs or other indicators of what is happening. We walk around the facility scouting for clues. We are here to learn and gather teachings, but about what?

We then decide to stop at the local convenience store and snoop around. At the counter I buy some drinking water and ask why they aren't selling Trinity water. The lady says they are closed in some kind of litigation. Outside, a line of customers is forming and I can tell the conversation is kept abrupt. There is a lack of cooperation in the area almost like we are intruding rather than looking for good water. On the side of the convenience store is an outfitter for water recreation so I poke in the doorway. A couple of young folks are working on equipment. I shift into a lost look and tell of our quest for folks at the Water facility. One of the young ladies perks up. She says "The way I hear it is that the Water Company was bought some six years back. Within the last year two major corporations came snooping around. They gathered information for legal loopholes. They found what they needed and proceeded to buy out the company. They're in litigation now and the operation had to close until the legal deeds got resolved. You might not find folks too friendly to talk about it."

I meander back to the truck and share my findings. The articles in environmental magazines about water being the 'new oil' are proving to be true. We decide to ride into Sun Valley, Idaho. I know my dreams are going to be busy, so after we arrive, we settle into a nice motel and I prepare for a night of teachings. I tell Dream Weaver, "Dream with the stars, not with the stories." Remember the principle "Truth gives Movement". The more truth, the more movement!

Shortly after I lie down and begin scanning my body for left over thoughts from the day that I hadn't processed. I roll over a few times getting comfortable while filing my thoughts. This is my ritual of getting through the fourth dimension. Once I get through, the fifth dimension descends upon me like a cloak of invisibility. Feeling the fifth dimension anchor in my dream reality, a floating like sensation lifts me out of any story-like interpretation. I stop thinking about what I am doing. The Elders are waiting as I find the sixth dimension at about 3 am.

The next morning, we sit in a local coffee shop and I share what I learned. The coffee is good! Paging through the local news, I find an article on Shamanism written by a local Seeker. Her studies were in the Peruvian tradition. I phone her leaving a message inviting her to meet us for coffee. When I return, a conversation has started with a lady about water. The information is the same as the day before. Dream Weaver makes some other calls on real estate listings and to other water bottlers in the area. Only one call is returned. We decide to spend the day scouting. The sun is shining and the green hues are awesome. We load up in the truck and drive north to Stanley, Idaho. During the trip we decide to be tourists. We stop at every highway pullout. We take pictures, enjoy the views and chat with other sightseers. Late that afternoon we return to Ketchum and go out to dinner. The restaurant is busy but Dream Weaver, Running Horse and I only wait for a few minutes. Running Horse is an old friend from North Dakota and has joined us for the day. He is traveling to Portland in the morning. As we wait for our orders all three of us are looking for some unseen voice. The level of sound is high already so it's like looking for nothing. It is Coyote! Coyote finally gets my attention. The message was that we have lost focus. I speak it out loud as a shame creeps over us.

This is evident by the loud voices rambling on about business, real estate transactions and general conquests while pouring the wine. Waitresses wearing skin-tight outfits offer us drinks in a flirting way while the rest of the ambiance is a modern day pirate's den. We are not in our element. When we come to this awareness, we leave. Coyote has tricked us. We have to shift back on our intent.

We decide to take a drive around Ketchum. What is beginning to be clear is this area is home to the rich and famous, and that these people can exist here out of the public eye. There are few middle and lower-class buildings. Most homes are high value. Coyote wants us to see this contrast. The area is clean, and people are friendly, and relationship to the surroundings was blended nicely. What is off balance? We drive over to Hailey, Idaho, which is only a few miles to the south. Here we find similar economic and housing issues. At one time the middle class had been here, but it was slowly being moved farther south. Why? It is true that many people from the film industry are in this area. The cover-up, surrounding the water and the image of caring for the earth is showing the hypocrisy of preaching global change, earth stewardship, and living in balance. Balance is represented in the way the buildings are colored, decorated and styled, yet it will take Mother Earth a number of years to grow the trees used for their construction. I wonder how many trees have been planted in return. We return to our motel and each go into the night dream.

Dream Weaver and I begin a discussion of recapitulation, which is a term Carlos Castenada writes about in his books. It describes a process by which a Seeker reflects back in time and charts a course of bringing the information into the present moment. By charting the course and adding circumstances, one can envision the lesson and the events, which are being magnetically drawn to the moment. My words are flying, as I think out loud "We had one return phone call out of eight real estate agents, one return phone call out of five water bottlers, illumination between classes of people, high living costs, beautiful land, lots of water and lots of holistic lifestyles in the area. Okay Grandmother, Grandfather, and Coyote, what is this journey about?" Mystery is beginning its wave around my body. I am still unclear about the trip to Sun Valley. We came on this trip scouting for land with water rights, comrades, community, and most of all a home. I have been searching for a home for a number of years. The sacred purpose that motivates my search is the preservation of teachings, lifestyle and ceremonial ground. We, as earth's guardians, need to be prepared to send prayers, during Coyote's romp around the globe.

Grandfather Eagle Heart taught me about the Seven Generations and Seven Fires Prophecy. He said every choice would effect seven generations before me and seven generations after me. The Monarch Butterfly reflects this in its migration from New England USA to South America. When the butterfly arrives at a migratory

destination it is seven generations removed from the original butterfly that started the journey. Recently I have wondered if the seven fires also represent the seven colors of the visual spectrum. This also correlates to the story of the seven seals in the book of Revelations of the Holy Bible. Seals may refer to the veils that separate out each layer of the human aura. When a seal breaks open, like an egg hatching, colors blend awakening coded messages in the DNA structure. The seals act as a guardian to the many dimensions of the spirit world. The colors of light could be the feminine principle of nature.

Dream Weaver begins interpreting from a technology perspective. "It's been known for some time how electromagnetic energies carry images of intent. These electromagnetic energies are increasing in their volume due to our web, internet-based technologies, and our use of cell phones, satellites and so forth. They create waves of information that are out of alignment with natural waves. Are these man made waves are creating conflict in space, or heavens?" Before there was an answer, Dream Weaver continues, "Didn't the Holy Bible speak of a war in the heavens? I thought it was in the past instead of now." I answer, "Yes, in the Book of Revelations. There are negotiations for the rights in space that could influence time. We see this on a daily basis in the paper with companies trying to buy frequencies on which to transmit their signals. Space and time could include the air, water, fire and earth. Eventually there will be a measure of value placed on the ability to send messages through the elements." Dream Weaver goes silent.

I continue, "Many Native people were killed and put in jail when they practiced their spiritual customs until the early 1970's. It was a felony to practice Ceremony, even to smoke a pipe. The constitutional rights like a freedom of religion and free speech didn't apply to Natives. When I asked Grandfather about these things he said, 'Prepare the seeds of knowledge to last the next Seven Generations of change.'"

Somewhere deep inside Dream Weaver and I share a sadness and betrayal. It is like the hope of abundance, happiness and a graceful life had been a lie. In spite of the emotions that are passing through, Coyote could be heard chuckling at the thought that we had just gotten seduced by the dark standard of living. Almost at the same time a new awareness opens. We have shared so many laughs and precious times on this quest that the fire of hope begins to burn bright within moments. The peaceful nights of rest are frequent as each Truth reveals itself. This is a great adventure!

Chapter 5 – Root

"All Intents Begin from the Center of the Circle"

Conifer, Colorado USA July 2006 A.D.

Star Blanket:

Grandmother Too Many Red Foxes speaks, "Star Blanket, you have been studying for several years. The coming changes on Earth are going to require some old friends from the animal world to be rebirthed. Remember back when you were a young man, you would sit on the riverbank and watch beaver for hours. Beaver would teach you how to build a container for living. Remember now."

I am falling, yet I know I am in a dream. Thump, I land with a sound that should hurt. Yep! In the night dream, looking around as the surroundings explode into my thoughts. I am on a riverbank on the Park River. I have been here many times since childhood. This river was my friend. It winds its way through Grafton, North Dakota, my birthplace. The river is my backyard. This spot is some three miles west out of town. The fall odors catch my attention as I look around. The high grass and fallen leaves that outline the riverbanks are brown adding a muddy color to the water. Harvested grain dust also fills the air.

Downstream a V-shaped ripple of water brings back memories of watching Muskrat, Mink and Beaver as they go about their chores. The locals call it Duck's Bend. As I lie on the bank there watching, Beaver comes into view. Beaver is heading for a u-shaped bend in the river. This formation provides a pond-like quality with mud and sand banks where many animals come to bathe, drink, and communicate, as a vision appears on the horizon across the river. Beaver is building a dam, and a large pond has developed. The water has expanded over grasslands, under trees and through the brush. In the dream the day turns to night and then into day. Many animals come to the water. There are winged ones, four leggeds, crawlers, and swimmers. The pond is a community center, vibrant twenty-four hours a day. The animals come to visit while gathering information by scouting the area. The water is awakened by their presence. The water becomes alive with coded information. Animals with their highly developed sensory skills can easily interpret the coded information. Beaver patrols the area attentive like a mother overlooking her children, but never interfering with any animal's activity. Remembering my youth, scouting wherever there was water, my senses were always enlivened when water was near.

A slight jerk puts me back into the night dream with Grandmother standing close by. She is smiling like many foxes that have visited the river. Our eyes meet in mutual respect and I start the journey back into the third dimension making sure not to rush. Slowly my body records the dream story with few distortions.

Lying in bed, the foggy images of the vision began to point to what will be needed to support the global changes. Water would be the link for global unification. The animals have been encoding and awakening water for years while humans are simultaneously destroying animals and their habitats of ponds, woodlands, air, lakes and streams. My thoughts seem to drift away except one. "It has been 10 years since I have started this journey of training apprentices in mystery schools while learning to be Star Blanket." Now is the time to finish this teaching cycle before beginning a new cycle of embodying my Elder medicine.

The phone rings near the bed as I put the final pinch of tobacco in the Sacred Pipe before going to sleep. An excited deep voice echoes. "Hello it's Wind Walker." It has been a few months since we have spoken. We have shared a parallel journey of being Mixed Bloods with hearts for the earth. The first time we met, I was sitting in a dentist's chair waiting to get my teeth x-rayed. Having been escorted to a treatment room, sitting down, I am looking right at a three-foot long ceremonial pipe hung mounted on the wall. I know instantly that power is lurking nearby. Continuing to settle in, Kachina dolls outlined the tops of partitions between stalls. A tall 6′ 5″ olive-skinned man in cowboy boots, Wrangler jeans and dental scrubs says "Hello" in a deep voice that is usually garnered for radio announcing. This is our first greeting. Now some 10 years later, we have become friends. The bond is not from sharing a lot of experiences together, but from a knowing deep inside. It is good to hear from him again.

After some pleasant greetings, Wind Walker suggests we do a vision quest together. Wind Walker thinks there is a connection between his involvement of sponsorsing a world-wide known researcher of water and my quest for learning the healing ways of water. Wind Walker says, "How about going four days. This could be helpful for us both!" He continues speaking, "I am deciding whether to do some Peace Corps type dentistry in Honduras and you are working with spiritual guidance on your quest to research water." I know there is a link between us so we decide to talk in a few days as our schedules unfold.

Later that day, I share Wind Walker's suggestion with Dream Weaver. The conversation eventually leads to the confusion of the two upcoming events. All the symptoms are of Coyote's trickery. One being the Annual Renewal Festival and the other is the vision quest that Wind Walker and I are planning. I say, "Let's understand the particulars of these different events before making any decisions. Besides it's not clear where these quests are going to take place." After a long discussion with Dream Weaver, we agree to hold the Renewal Festival in Colorado and remain open to the possibility of another location showing up for the Wind Walker quest. Within a few minutes of hanging up the phone, a wave of drifting into alternate dream spaces comes flooding. The first wave passes quickly. The drifting sensation pauses as my body adjusts to the glow of the fifth dimension. Grandmother Too Many Red Foxes is waiting! "Quest to the southwest, where the Cloud Spirit visits. Wander with the rolling stone, until we contact you." With a nodding "HO!" she is gone and I continue daydreaming.

My body glows as if adjusting to resting on a plateau. Eventually looking around I see Beaver. Beaver is working on a home for the winter. The freshly cut wood embalms the cool air. Beaver turns and speaks by sending thought pictures towards me. The thoughts translate into my own language and are filtered by my imprinting. Beaver says, "My purpose is simple, I network as I scout wood for my home. The patterns of flowing water I create assist the circle of life everywhere. Be like the water on your quest. Do not stop to be a pond, except to rest." Beaver turns back to the home that is being built. There are no more transmissions. Looking around, familiar symbols from my bedroom come into my daydream. As always when communicating from the sixth to eighth dimension, words are a nuisance. Moving slowly, the interpretation becomes clear. By mid morning the vision's message is clear. The Renewal Festival is taking place in a week. Hosting the Renewal is like building a pond for the forest's inhabitants. The building has to continue despite the seductions of getting involved with people's process of transformation. The Renewal Festival would be a building block to the Wandering Vision Quest. Each is a Circle within itself and preparations must be complete before I could be mindless on Wind Walker's Vision Quest.

Beginning the Quest from a centered question is the seed of the principle Grandmother wants us to practice. Telephoning Wind Walker and sharing Grandmother's message, we agree to head towards Pagosa Springs and Durango, Colorado. Later that day he e-mails the travel plans. He will arrive in two weeks. I begin packing for the Renewal Festival.

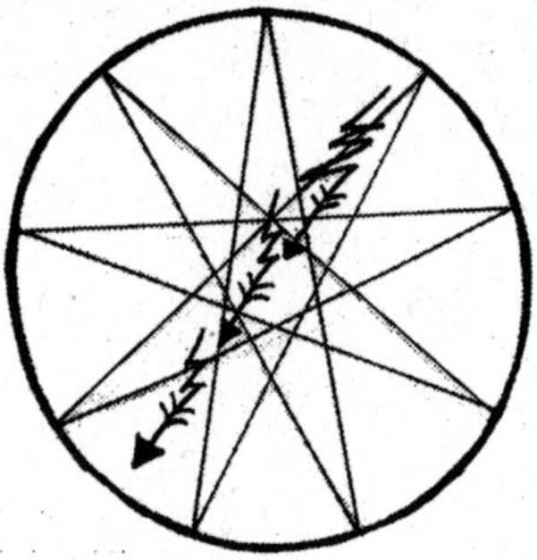

First Annual Renewal Festival

Star Blanket:

Tuesday morning during this preparatory week, after coffee and running a mile up and down a steep hill behind my home, I relax in my easy chair. Within moments I am remembering a dream from a year ago. The dream about the Renewal Festival was during my "pregnancy" two years ago. Pregnancy is my term for a 15-month initiation in dream training. Grandmother Too Many Red Foxes, Grandfather Buffalo Heart and other spirits without names had visited me for many nights. At the time, these Elders expressed their desire for an annual gathering, which would be called a Renewal Festival.

Grandmother Too Many Red Foxes had spoken, "An annual gathering will provide containment for all symbols and the knowledge represented to transfer. This gathering will provide all the reflections of the strengths and challenges that global unification faces. This is the way. Braids can be woven from the wisdom that each Seeker opens. Humans often avoid direct intimacy, so by creating an event provides a stepping-stone towards resolution of separation. This is magic of the third dimension. Like the beaver creating a pond, the Renewal Festival will create the interrelatedness. Always keep the circle open." With those words she was gone. Suddenly in my living room looking around at familiar decorations I come back into present time. Coyote's breath is present. Something is intensifying, I think.

The days leading up to the Renewal Festival are mixed with emotions, memories and teachings I have lived by. About three days before the group of nine are to arrive, my emotions clear. Soon after crawling into bed, I pass through the fifth dimension to communicate with the Spirit world that guides me. Grandmother Too Many Red Foxes meets me and smiles as she turns revealing a large fire near a tall rock inlet. The rocks are gleaming with the shadows of a council. Elders sit wrapped in blankets of mixed colors. Painted and sewn symbols on their blankets tell of their heritage and medicine they gift to the Circle. Grandmother motions me to sit and listen to the discussion. An Elder is speaking about Earth being the gathering Circle for many spirits that need to complete their lessons. He is saying that nowadays incarnated Spirits have forgotten their purpose. Too Many Red Foxes responds, looking in my direction, "The earth is mostly water, the movement is in place to awaken the forgotten memory through the waters, land and sky. This council dreams for many Keepers of the Ways. It is time for the weaving and sharing of wisdom within the Mixed Bloods. Many Mixed Bloods will join organized movements as well as unorganized. Natural laws will dictate the speed. This will regenerate the Sky Women's Web of unity." Grandmother turns away and slowly lets her words sink in as she meets each Elder's eyes. They all nod in agreement. Grandmother turns to me and says, "You know what to do!" Standing up I begin to say thank you. In a blink of an eye, I am back in my bedroom pondering the images and possible feelings of what Sky Women's Web of unity could be.

Dream Weaver:
Star Blanket had suggested we should prepare for a Renewal Festival. It is more of an assignment than a suggestion. I've come to learn the difference between suggestions for something that I might want to look into, and assignments that would be containers for illuminations of internal battles. This particular time I know I am being asked to enter into an initiation, only I am not sure what this is going to entail. I know something is up. I am not sure what I know, but I know enough to trust and have faith that Spirit will take care of me. I jump on the opportunity to help produce the Renewal Festival. It is going to be another medicine journey, and that's all I need to know. This medicine journey will allow me to experience the Circle inside and outside of myself at the same time. I will be playing multiple roles, and will have to jump between multiple realities. I am helping to produce the event, I will participate as a Seeker on Ceremony, and I will assist Star Blanket in monitoring others while they are on Ceremony. Needless to say, there is quite a bit that going on!

We originally thought this event would take place in Colorado. Logically and logistically that would be the most convenient location. Since we will be providing supplies for people we think it should be someplace we can drive to, it should be a remote location so people could go on Ceremony, and be readily available by airport for those folks coming from out of state. Colorado seems to fit all of the requirements, but there is something about the location that isn't sitting right with me. It feels like we are somehow forcing the location instead of the location telling us it wants to have us there. The place we had found was in a state park in Colorado, and participants had already booked their airfares to Denver. I still feel like some other mystery will reveal itself. That is the way of Coyote. Star Blanket calls while I am deep in thought. He says "Let's go down to

Denver for supplies." I agree.

It is about a week and a half before our Renewal Festival. As we gather food staples, blankets, propane and other supplies Star Blanket proceeds to tell me about a phone call he has received from White Eagle. She is the medicine Keeper of the Origin Teachings of the Delicate Lodge, a body of knowledge that moves through the indigenous people of the Americas. Hers is also a mixed blood and Métis path. Star Blanket and White Eagle have been friends for some time. They discovered that they both were going to be taking people out on Ceremony during the same week! While Star Blanket is relaying his conversation with White Eagle to me, I suggest that we do our Renewal Festival together with White Eagle's group on her land in New Mexico. We both look at each other and start laughing. At once, the Sequoia is filled with an echo of Coyote's howling. A year ago on another journey, Star Blanket had taken a group of folks including myself to the Village of the Shining Stones for their opening ceremonies. That is the name of the land that White Eagle's teachers steward. As Star Blanket and I are sitting in his car, with the click of his cell phone, he calls White Eagle again, and asks about the possibility of doing such a journey together. She agrees. It is set! The First Annual Renewal Festival is going to take place in the Village of the Shining Stone. People will still fly into Denver and we will all drive down to White Eagle's land together.

From then on, Star Blanket and I begin talking every day. It is now a week before the Renewal Festival. Many people from all parts of the United States have indicated interest in the Festival. As with many things in life, the initial excitement is contagious. I am reminded of the mind games that we play as the time for the Renewal Festival gets closer and closer. Every excuse available is expressed as people go into their bargaining process. As with my ceremonies, there is a point when I realize my own trickster. It will be now at this point when many folks will bail out because they just aren't ready. The bargaining will come in many forms. The excuses look like 'I don't have enough money' or 'I have a big deadline at work that week that I really can't miss' or 'I just found out that is the week I'm supposed to be at Great Aunt Emmie's 90th birthday'. It doesn't matter how it looks it is all the same thing. This is Coyote's way of testing us as to who is willing to engage in the Festival experience. Of the 23 people that indicated interest, 11 people have confirmed their attendance.

The day to leave arrives and we pack the rig. The high Desert in northern New Mexico will be hot. It is the end of July. The Sequoia is full with seven people from across the country. The attached cargo trailer has all the supplies for cooking, camping and Ceremony. Star Blanket and I have also added several cases of Awakened Water from a Ceremony that happened two days before this departure. Awakened Water is the name given to the state of water after being blessed in a ceremonial way. Water is a precious resource in the desert. Some of the Awakened Water is intended as a medicine gift to White Eagle and the rest for drinking. It is an eight-hour drive and we check into the Abiquiu Inn late at night. I am appreciating my last shower at the Inn as I prepare for the last leg of our journey in the morning, to the site for our First Annual Renewal Festival.

After a breakfast of eggs and green chili we head towards the Village of the Shining Stones. It is a sunny day and already the temperature is heating up. Our group is quiet this morning. Four others will be meeting us there during the week. We find the road that winds its way around the Abiquiu reservoir. It is a beautiful area but looks very empty and desolate. The land we are entering is so fragile and survival here will require efficiency of energy use. The land itself is a place where tribes agreed to have no battles. Obsidian, a mineral used for knives and other forms of cutting throughout the area could be found even though it is not indigenous to the area.

White Eagle meets us at the entrance of the land. She is a brunette, with hair down past her shoulders, about 5′ 10″ tall, slim, very pretty and focused. We pile out of the air-conditioned Sequoia into the now 90-degree day. We are literally in the middle of nowhere. White Eagle welcomes us and after name exchanges and greetings she gives us a brief orientation of the land. The land is flat on the eastern side with a large canyon gorge running along the west border. The pinion trees are short and rough. There are short cacti sticking out all over the ground with 2-inch thorns on them. The rocks are dry and crumbly, like hardened sand. They hold the stories of the heat cycles that play out each day and the cold chills at night. As the temperature drops there is nothing to hold the heat. I'm wondering to myself, "How am I ever going to make it a week out here?" I'm not fond of broiling-type heat and here I am in the middle of the desert. I try to look at it as an opportunity to get to know an ecosystem that I've never spent any time in.

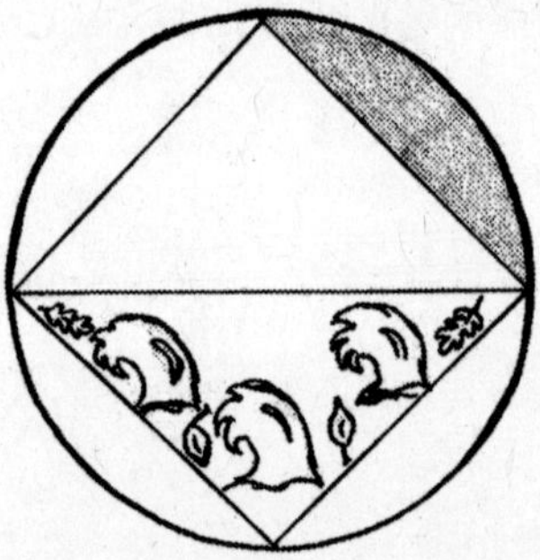

As we are walking I notice how much crypto biotic soil there is. It is dirt that is made up of tiny living microorganisms that create filaments throughout the soil. It joins loose soil particles together into a web and helps prevent erosion by making the surface more resistant to wind and water erosion. Like the light reflecting off of stars creating a symbol of Sky Women's Web, the Earth has a web of efficiency. It is ancient, and takes hundreds and hundreds of years to grow. The crypto biotic soil helps make Earth's air. It is incredibly fragile and tends to grow in deserts and tundra. Just touching it, or stepping on it, kills it. I am trying to walk from rock to rock as to not damage it. We will have an enormous impact on this land, even under the best of circumstances, even with all the care and love we all have for Mother Earth. As we continue on our orientation, White Eagle gives us a lesson on water conservation. Since it has to be trucked in, there isn't much of it, so we must use it sparingly and judiciously. The land is a work in progress for the community vision White Eagle is working with. There is an outdoor camping kitchen. Alongside are the showers and storage areas. There are three port-a-potties and the first structures on the land are open-air showers. The water heaters and showers are run by a generator. As I get used to the quiet of the land, the sound of the generator starting up is like a jet engine. Quite a contrast! The people that are studying with White Eagle join us as we walk through the area.

Star Blanket picks a little used driveway to park and set up the camp kitchen. As our gear is laid out, our people gather their packs and set out to pitch tents and dig trenches for the possible rains that can downpour. Star Blanket asks me to assist wherever I am needed before setting up my tent. This will be my first Ceremony where I will monitor, a far cry from where I was at the Sunlight Dance over 2 years ago. I am going to be experiencing and learning from the Keeper position (or the West) on the Medicine Wheel during this Renewal Festival. My role is to allow images attached to energy to pass through my body while I convert the energy back to the participant by letting go of the images. Loosely translated this means that most of what people experience will flow towards me for sorting. I can tell that my Initiation is starting because I am full of self-doubt. Will I be able to keep a clear intent to hold the space for people who have trained with Star Blanket for over 10 years? Am I really able to sense the Spirits and the energy and know its meaning? I know that I will be challenged in many ways, but I also know it is perfect. I'm learning how to be in a proactive mode instead of a reactive mode. As we settle in, it feels like we're intruding on the land. I wonder if my European ancestors felt this same way when they arrived in America.

There are two Keepers of the Ways here, Star Blanket and White Eagle. They hold Bundles of Knowledge in the form of Braided Traditions. White Eagle's Bundle was granted to her after numerous years of apprenticeship. Star Blanket's was under many teachers, modalities and the karmic journey of being a Lone Eagle. His Bundle is from physical accomplishments also but was granted in the metaphysical dream world. There will be a weaving of Bundles taking place on many levels at this First Renewal Ceremony.

My thoughts continue to wander as we scout to find where to set up tents and where to leave belongings while out on Ceremony. We set up the tipi, which will hold the Mesa (alter) and Lineage Pipe while everyone is out on Ceremony. The tipi will also be used for two naming ceremonies.

I start setting up my own tent. It is midday, and the temperature is breaking 100 degrees. The fine desert sand is sticking to my sweat. The element of fire will become one of the tyrants. The desert can really test patience, when you are hot, sweaty, covered in sand, and thirsty. My thoughts are, "This ain't no vacation," and yet, I am so happy.

We all move slowly to help our bodies adjust to the heat and to become more efficient in adjusting to the limited water supply. The electromagnetic energy fields from the city are dropping off our bodies from the computers, cell phones, ipods, etc. The spirit of the land is making its way into all of us. We are dreaming with the land. Of the six participants, three people are going out today on a 48-hour Ceremony and one person is doing an overnight. There will be two types of Vision Quests. Star Blanket and I will be monitoring the questers during that time from the camper trailer base camp, meaning that we will establish a connection with the people in Ceremony. This way, we will be able to energetically support them if need be.

We have set up the outside kitchen. It is just outside the cargo trailer. The inside of the trailer also has a small kitchen and folding beds which have been set up inside. The remaining participants will be arriving over the next two days and will be going out on overnights and multi-day Ceremonies. There is a lot to coordinate to make sure that everyone is taken care of and safe. I am now understanding how much emotional, physical, mental, and spiritual focus is required to keep the intent sacred for this many people, especially in this harsh environment. Every thought will mean something. I will have to be clear about my own personal feelings so that I can be fully available to the others and what they will be going through.

The first people to go out on Ceremony are the advanced students. They have been studying with Star Blanket as long, or much longer than I. I sense their experience by the choice to climb down the rocky slope into the river valley. Thunderbird Woman, Crystal Pathfinder, and Whirlwind all build their Medicine Wheel circles for Vision Questing in remote locations. It has been agreed that because of the severe weather, Star Blanket or I will bring a gallon of Awakened Water down once a day with some snacks. It's a lesson for me to realize how sometimes the simplest of things can make a big difference to someone.

Everyone except Jaguar Woman is out in the desert. This is her first time camping. She is a little apprehensive and decides to go to her tent early that evening. There is just Star Blanket and I left awake. Star Blanket gives me teachings on monitoring using the Lineage Pipe. He begins by saying to fly over the canyon with an Eagle's viewpoint scanning for movement and contrasts in sensations. I am trying to be confident as I listen, but this is my first night of sharing all this responsibility. Star Blanket continues teaching while cooking spaghetti.

A thunderstorm with sky-to-ground lightening is moving rapidly through the canyon, giving an amazing light and sound show. Star Blanket says, "The Thunderbirds are coming". We check in to how everyone is handling the weather and feel satisfied about all the Seekers' safety. Star Blanket stays in the trailer while I walk outside. As I return to the trailers doorway, a bolt of lightening crashes into the ground 50 yards from me. I literally fly into the trailer with my eyes opened in fear so wide, that they almost popped from my head. I practically land into Star Blanket's arms. He is laughing so hard that I have to start laughing too, even as my hair is standing up on end. The sound is loud and electric energy radiates throughout the land. Mother Nature is teaching. Lightening is fire and air. When uniting these elements with earth and water we get enormous energy vibrations. Star Blanket says, "The evening will be interesting." With a turn he goes back to cooking.

Star Blanket and I stay up talking late into the night. He tells me that if I feel any energy coming that I should go smoke the Grandmother's Return Lineage pipe that is setup on the Mesa in the tipi. The Elders will share through the Sacred Pipe what is going on and with whom. If it is something serious, I should come get him. Nervous about the responsibility I go into the Dreamtime and get up once during the night and smoke the pipe. My doubt has crept in to my thoughts and I want to be sure there are no problems. It is a fifty-yard walk to the tipi. I stop at the bathroom on the way. The door seems to send a creaking sound through the whole canyon, as I try to be silent. The canyon seems very calm. Everyone is doing okay. I go back and lie down in my tent. I am learning to trust my instinct.

Jaguar Woman is going out on an overnight quest. There will be five people out on Ceremony now. Star Blanket and I make our way down the canyon in the early afternoon shortly after Jaguar Woman leaves to set up her site. We carry the water and snacks for the others that are already out on Ceremony. As we hike down the steep rocks, a torrential downpour begins. Star Blanket and I find shelter under a large boulder and I begin babbling. "This is a land of extremes. It is either boiling hot, freezing cold, or pouring rain." The sides of the boulder rocks and crevices turn to waterfalls and rivers within a matter of minutes. The temperature drops rapidly. We left the trailer in 100-degree heat under a sunny sky. I had instinctively grabbed my rain jacket and backpack. I pull out my rain jacket. Star Blanket starts laughing and says, "You're learning."

There are four women and one man. We quietly approach each person in his or her Medicine Wheel. Then we call out making sure each person has some time to adjust to our presence. We keep our conversations brief so we don't disturb what is taking place, and drop off some Awakened drinking water. Each person thanks us for hiking down in the downpour to bring water. This land is a vulnerable place to be. Learning to depend on someone at their word is learning trust and faith. It is here that I once again realize how intimacy comes in many forms. To know that people have put their trust and faith in us helps me understand how much my word means. It actually brings me to tears thinking back to the times when I thought that our words were just that, words. I am getting the full experience in my body realizing that words are putting energy out, and energy is everything.

Later that evening, Star Blanket and I are the only two at camp. Everyone is out on Ceremony. We join White Eagle for dinner at her camp kitchen. The sun is setting and creating a glow over the canyon. It is a glow of bright red-orange neon with silvery faces weaving in the clouds. These are known as Kachina-hey or Dream Teachers. The entire sky changes before our eyes and the land becomes silent. The wind stops, not a single sound can be heard. We all stop eating, get up and walk to the open sky to get a full view of what is happening. It is breathtaking as colored streaks fill the entire sky. I grab my camera from my pocket and snap a picture of Star Blanket and White Eagle with the sky in the background. We all look at it in the back of the digital camera in silence, there are no words required. The Bundles of the two

Keepers are being woven together. There is a peace throughout the area like I have never felt. I go to bed with a knowing, but cannot find the words to explain. I sleep even though I am still on duty monitoring! My confidence in converting energy is increasing.

The next morning, I am lying in my tent when I hear Star Blanket lightly drumming. It is for me I thought. When I hear the drum, I am being called. My eyes are opening as I hear the beat of the drum. I am answering the call but talking to myself saying, "I hear you, I hear you, I'm coming." I get up, open my tent and put my boots on to hike the short trail to where the trailer is. I am about half way up the trail when I see Star Blanket coming down with a coffee for me in his hand and saying, "Good Morning." "I heard you drumming," I say, "I was on my way up." He smiles at me and hands me a coffee saying, "Dream Weaver, I wasn't drumming. It must be the Ancestors from the land who were drumming." Star Blanket turns around, starts walking back up the trail and then turns towards me and says, "Looks like you're going to have an interesting Ceremony. Find your center before you begin otherwise Coyote will find you entertaining." I go back to my tent with my coffee, gather my things and prepare for my own Vision Quest.

Chapter 6 - Trunk

"Birthing has a Minimum of Three Intents"

Abiquiu, New Mexico USA July 2006 A.D.

Dream Weaver:
With only a sleeping bag and a tarp, I head out down the unmarked canyon trail alone. I find my spot to set up my Circle. From past experience I know that my Circle has to have enough room to move around in since I will spend the next 48 hours in it. This spot is on an overlook of the canyon where I can watch the birds fly in the updrafts. There are some rock formations to sit on, and a pinion tree. I am doing the calling in of the Ancestors within my Circle. Something odd catches my eye. I look down to find a weathered slide rule in a leather case lying in the dirt, in the perfect North of my Circle. The North direction, among other things, is the direction of Mental of our teachings on Human Aspects. I look around to see if someone is playing a joke. I immediately hear Star Blanket's words about Coyote. "Find your Center before you begin or else Coyote would find you very entertaining," he had said.

I haven't taken enough time to transition from monitoring to doing my own Ceremony. Coyote is going to be here as an

Ancestor Spirit. I let out a relieving sigh.

After some mind play, I decide to set my intents! I want to become connected to the land and dedicated to expanding into the area. I set an intent that every time I take a drink of water from my precious resource, I will give a drink to the land. One for me, one for the ancestors I speak as I practice. For a moment, fear sets in, as worry about running out of water passes through my mind. The thought passes quickly as I know that Spirit is taking care of me.

Very soon I watch the canyon walls as the sun fades away. The Thunderbird clouds are moving in. I can see the storm coming from miles away. My mind is racing with thoughts. "I hope it is quick", but I can tell that the blanket of clouds is more then just a passing shower. I take my tarp and wrap it around my sleeping bag. I lie down in the middle of my Circle as the rain starts to fall. I just make it. As the quiet settles in to my Circle I hear everyone at camp singing and drumming. This goes on for about an hour. I am glad that everyone is having fun drumming. It is one of my favorite things to do. Then thunder and lightning crash and boom over my head. It rains all night long and doesn't stop until morning. I stay awake the entire night, turning on my Internal Fire to keep warm. While it is very cold outside my sleeping bag turns into a big, orange sponge. I never feel too cold although I am soaking wet. Ah! I scream "Coyote go away. I get it." YEH!

Star Blanket and Thunderbird Woman arrive late in the day to bring my water ration. Thunderbird Woman has taken over assisting plus monitoring. We all chat briefly and I tell them it was nice to listen to everyone drumming and singing last night. Once again, Star Blanket says, "We weren't drumming or singing." We all silently nod in awareness of the spirit world revealing itself as I am thinking it is something else. After a brief moment I pull out the slide rule and they both roll their eyes. I ask "What are the chances of finding this in the middle of the Desert and then in my Circle?" I continue, "Pretty good for an engineer!"

As I watch them leave loneliness begins to set in. I won't see anyone for another twenty four hours. Coyote seems to grab my mind as the thoughts spiral. The slide rule is measure for my learning which is perfect since I am measuring my learning in all areas of my life. I have gathered knowledge in the manmade world, often with great conflict. The natural world is now revealing the measure between the former reality and this natural reality. I had set the intent for attuning to the land. The Spirit world brought me this slide rule.

As I look around, the trunk of a nearby Juniper tree catches my eye. I realize at once that the Trunk of the tree is nature's slide rule for the harmony between realities. My skills as an engineer are humbled by nature's skill level. I am Free Dancing this Ceremony, which means it is totally unstructured except for the design of the medicine wheel. There is no protocol to follow. I spend hours just sitting, listening, and watching what is going on around me, getting reflections of what is going on inside me. After some timeless sitting I look down to find ants. I have built my Medicine Wheel around a small anthill. How did I miss that yesterday, I ask out loud? Memories of being lost in my Sunlight Ceremony flood my head as my disappointment spreads. I must have been walking on their home for the last twenty-four to forty hours. I want to cry. There are many anthills on the land, some being 60-70 years old. It is a microcosm of the macrocosm, a mirror of how all the worlds live together. I scream inside myself as Coyote laughs nearby. I sink into despair at the thought of my destruction.

By the time I come out of the mirror of my destruction, it is scorching hot again. The soaked sleeping bag is now dry and draped over my head to keep the Sun from beating down on me. I am sitting on the sand, watching as the ants scurry about. It looks like total chaos, yet it is completely choreographed. All of the ants, maybe 50 at a time, emerge from this little hole. It first appears that they are aimlessly running back and forth from the hole to the end of the mound and then back to the hole. How efficient, I think, there is no energy wasted. This is a non-stop process. It is amazing that their little bodies don't burn up from the heat of the land! Each ant emerges from the anthill with a tiny spec of sand which it has gathered from inside the tunnel. The ants never collide. They do this in total synchronization. All emerge, all return at the same time. There is no competition. They all work for the good of the whole. I wonder if they get thirsty. One insight I get from the ant is patience. They remind me that when everything around me appears to be in chaos it really is in perfect order. It takes me back to the lesson that all battles are with the self. How many times have I tried to make sense of chaos when it fact it was the acceptance of the inherent order that I needed. I watch these ants until the sun goes down.

The night turns to morning. The first yip of coyotes crosses the canyon. Within seconds, all of the other members of the pack respond with their own howls. They are directly across the canyon and I feel as if they are howling a morning song. I sit for a couple of hours as the sun comes up and lights the canyon walls. Then walking across the sealed perimeter of my Medicine Wheel, undoing the energy, I gather each rock and take them to a new resting place. I realize that I've brought a part of this environment inside me and think back to the beginning of the week when I was wondering whether or not I would be able to be in the desert for the week. I laugh and start howling back across the canyon with the Coyotes.

It is time to pack out. I begin stuffing my tarp and sleeping bag into my backpack, gather my slide rule, and notice I still have water left. I think back to how nervous I was about giving half my water to the land. Now I am holding the bottle realizing that I always have enough. I am free to share what I have once there is no attachment. I put my backpack on and hike up the canyon. I pause one last time before emerging out of the canyon to thank the ancestors and the land for once again letting me find another part of myself.

As I walk, carrying my pack, I remember not to draw conclusions from my personal Ceremony. The revelations will come over the next weeks and months and I will get glimpses of different aspects of what had happened while at the Renewal Festival. The weaving of the Bundles that occurred allowed sharing of knowledge, customs, and teachings. Something special has happened and an adventurous mystery is unfolding. Spirit is growing the seeds of this last week and Coyote is making sure they are honored. Coyote, the trickster, has proven to be an ally and tricked me back onto the right trail, even when I wanted a different one.

I reach camp and Star Blanket is waiting with a grin and hot coffee. I am exhausted yet want no sleep. He says we are doing two naming ceremonies that afternoon and that I am to find Whirlwind to practice chant numbers eighteen and eleven. He turns to leave and then looks back. "I had a visit from an old spirit guide last night that was assigned to me years ago. He goes by the name of Buffalo Heart." Chills run up and down my spine like a lightning bolt had just been thrown at me. I waver in my stance. Star Blanket's grin widens as he walks away. I think, "He is getting more like Coyote every day."

Two names are given in a beautiful Ceremony in Star Blanket's tipi that afternoon. Whirlwind and I lead the chants while Star Blanket receives the visions for the names. All seems to be peaceful. A council is to take place the next morning between the two camps, Bundles and their Keepers. The focus is on the preservation of the teachings, ceremonial alchemy and how business models could learn from within these ancient ways. As I walk around the land I know I need rest. Many of the folks in our camp are preparing for sleep or going off to be alone. It is a time for taking care of personal needs. I decide to go to bed.

I awake to the sun baking the inside of my tent. I know Star Blanket will have fried potatoes cooking. He has this tradition of cooking potatoes with pieces of fruit and seasoning. It is his way of honoring the ancestors from his agricultural lineage's in North America to South America. I roll out of the sleeping bag and prepare for the day. When I arrive at the kitchen, Jaguar Woman and Whirlwind have made coffee and pancakes and of course there are potatoes. After breakfast, Star Blanket pulls me aside. He says, "Pay close attention today while we are in council. The Thunderbirds have been talking the last few nights about the future of these two Bundles. The message will not be in the words, but in what is not said. I need you to monitor like a scribe so I can feel free to express some concerns. You have done this before, Weaver." Chills ran through me like the day before. He leaves me like that and as I walk to the bathroom I remember saying a couple of years ago that I will write about these ways some day. That must be what he meant by "Weaver."

We gather by the community kitchen. Seating is in a circle with folks sitting randomly except that I notice nobody has sat next to White Eagle. Star Blanket arrives and goes directly to the seat across from her. I then sit next to her like it is already planned. The Talking Stick is passed with formal introductions and White Eagle expresses the intent of the council. After the round of introductions each person gives their views of what they had heard from the land and what future the land wanted. It is generally agreed that indeed it is for Ceremony. There are many discussions about how to make money while living this lifestyle. All seems to go fairly smooth except that "money making" feels interruptive to the peaceful feeling of the last week. Talk about business and profit seems to bring back an element of stress. I feel myself drifting somewhere when I hear Star Blanket speak in a distinct tone, "We are deciding a future today that can be conflictual for Medicine Keepers. I hear today what the Keepers should do with legal entities, marketing and making the knowledge available. What I don't hear is what people are willing to give. Business models are fine for business people, but if Keepers have to do that work their medicine craft suffers. Keepers and Guardians of these ways need to be taken care of in the business realms so they can keep their medicine sharp during the coming changes on this planet. If I spend my time promoting and trying to become a credible Shaman in magazines, who attends to the land and the youth who want to learn?" The group goes silent and awkward as if they were just scolded. White Eagle suggests a break. Everyone agrees.

The council continues after the break and is split in loyalties between the preservation of knowledge for profit and the preservation for lifestyle. We close with another round of viewpoints and it is obvious that Star Blankets words had found some hearts. As I walk back to our main camp I think about the council. This split in out hearts has been going on for hundreds of years. Why do I know the argument so well?

The next morning we have a closing Circle, pack up and begin our journey back to Conifer, Colorado. Star Blanket drives while doing his best to keep us from processing out loud. He doesn't want to distort any information by talking before some integration time. Crystal Pathfinder is staying an extra two days in Conifer and will help Star Blanket clean up all the camping gear. We are all very quiet on the drive. It has been a big week with much to think about. I have a lot of weaving to do!

Star Blanket:

Wind Walker arrives a week after we return home for our

wandering Vision Quest. The Sequoia is ready for another journey. It seems that my medicine name Star Blanket is taking hold in my body, for teachings in the dream time and ceremonies are more frequent. Wind Walker and I are full of excitement as we turn the Rhino south on highway 285 heading towards Pagosa Springs, Colorado. Our conversations range from personal relationships to interfacing universal principles to gospel teachings of original writing of the Holy Bible. Our first night and opening pipe Ceremony will be on Wolf Creek pass, some 10,000ft above sea level, between South Fork and Pagosa Springs Colorado. We arrive shortly before dark, build a fire and set up sleeping sites next to towering ponderosa pine trees.

The fire is warm as our conversations edge their way to setting up intent. I begin to speak first. "I am seeking guidance about a dream concerning the awakening of healing codes in water and about a gathering place where Elders can visit and pass on their knowledge into the water." Wind Walker looks at me puzzled. I immediately explain, "During the fifteen month pregnancy a vision of water bubbling out of the earth was given to me. There were many parts to the vision that included teachings from many lifetimes about the use of water as a carrier of coded messages. One part of the vision still eludes me. What I understand so far is that many spiritual leaders and medicine people would be willing to pass on their knowledge in a coded form. The reason for the codes is that only the evolved humans with a heart for the future well being of Earth would be able to access the knowledge from the water. Water would become a collective library. What I seek is the course of action to implement this vision." I stop talking while Wind Walker takes the concept in. After some quiet moments he nods, showing his understanding.

"What is your intent for this Quest" I ask? Wind Walker begins, "I am looking for guidance for some dreams I been having about the science of dentistry going into Central America. I feel it is my time to give back what I have been given." We both go silent and as if on cue I add, "And the third is how the two intents are related." Wind Walker nods a yes. We soon dose out the fire and find our areas where tarps are tied to the trees for covering. It will snow tonight, but we want to be in the open air with the stars and the sounds of the creek rushing nearby. We want dreaming!

The next morning Wind Walker and I decide that this Quest will be wandering to gather information in symbolic form around the four corners area. Like a couple of animals marking their territory, we hike into the mountains to do some fly fishing and integrate last nights dreaming. Our plan is to camp below Chimney Rock and then drive on to Durango, Shiprock New Mexico and Ouray, Colorado the next night. Our journey is about 200 miles long circling the Four Corners region. When we arrive at Ouray, Colorado we are worn down with driving, talking and processing the many visions we share. None of the visions stand out in clarity, but are related like a string of beads. It is clear that this Quest's answers would show up later.

We check into a motel in Ouray that has geothermal hot tubs. The hot tubs are old-style wine barrels which were built into landscaped decking that latticed itself up the mountain side. The water flows through the eight to ten tubs on a continuous basis. As Wind Walker and I go out to a local steak house, the conversation starts to lean towards the use of sexual energy on the planet and how it is becoming an entertainment-type value. We have a very intense talk about many spiritual traditions that unite male and female energy as a creative force. The discussion continues all the way back to the motel. While we soak in the hot tubs for a couple of hours, and then before going to bed, we decide we'd better turn this over to the Spirit world. The question that we cannot resolve is how much of that creative sexual energy is used to encode water in the old ways. By midnight we are in the night dreams.

The phone rings early near my bed. Through sleepy eyes it seems like it is Dream Weaver on the caller ID. Answering, I say,

"Hello and what are you doing calling this early?" Laughing she responds "It's Karma for the all the times you've called me while I was sleeping." Dream Weaver continues, "I just got a call about a hot springs retreat that has just come back on the market in central Colorado. It's the same property we had seen in a real estate listing a few months back. Is it possible for the two of you to stop there on the way back to Denver?" Thinking about Wind Walkers departure later in the afternoon I say, "Yes, we can be there by noon." Dream Weaver says, "I'll set it up," and she is gone. Turning to the sleepy giant who is in his bed I relay the message. Almost at once we get out of the blankets and begin getting ready. We both know this is the highlight of the trip. Within an hour we are on the highway.

Within a few minutes of noon, the Rhino pulls into the retreat. It is built in western dude ranch architecture, carved into the mountain. There is a swimming pool and an adjoining hot tub that were both fed by geothermal water. Wind Walker and I are given a walk through the grounds by one of the owners. She feels like a grandma taking her lost grandsons through her life's work. When we are almost finished walking, we find ourselves near the source of the geothermal water coming out of the earth. One of the groundskeepers calls out from the main cabin announcing to grandma that she is wanted on the phone. She excuses herself. The break gives Wind Walker and me a chance to talk and dream into the water's source without being rude to her. Extending our energy intent into the water, images form quickly. A minute seems like an hour. Wind Walker turns and says, "I see it." He is talking about the Elders blessing the water which I am watching as well. Our trance is interrupted by grandma returning. She looks at us in a knowing way!

After some pleasant closing conversation we depart from the retreat's plaza. The four-hour ride to Denver is lively with talk. The answers to the intents we had sent out on this quest are not clear yet. We are sure that the information is available in our bodies now and that the mystery will reveal itself in the coming months. Wind Walker and I both feel complete with our quest and are excited about the mystery ahead. I think as I leave the airport that we are on different paths in this life and yet the paths will cross from time to time. I feel no void in our friendship. An hour later I arrive at my home. Getting out my gear, I discover Wind Walker has left his cell phone in the Sequoia. Coyote is having some fun with him.

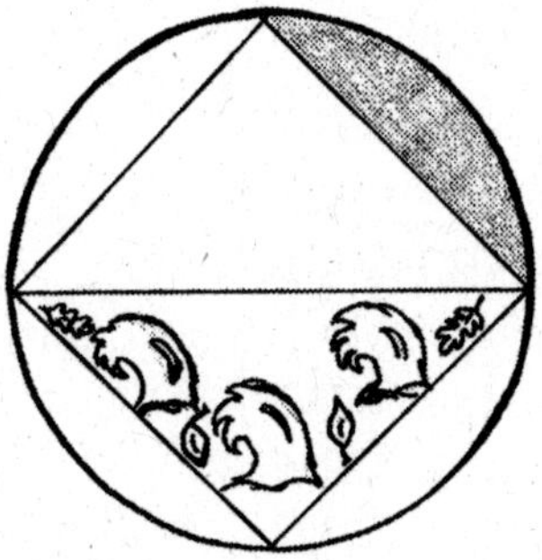

Chapter 7—Budding

"Ally the Power of Death"

Conifer, Colorado 2007 A.D.

Star Blanket:

"It's been a month since Wind Walker and I went on the vision quest. We have spoken once since our departure at the airport. Wind Walker has shared his chaotic re-entry into northern Idaho. Coyote has made the journey home long so he could integrate.

The information slows down during the last two weeks. Dream Weaver and I wait for the next movement.

Saturday morning sunlight peeks through the medicine blanket covering the bedroom window. Coyote is hanging around my aura, nudging a cold spirit nose for me to get moving. The Spirit world has been dogging me for a few days to keep writing. I am exhausted finding meaning with some teenage memories which have surfaced. I have just completed putting all the magnetic pieces together yesterday and I don't feel like spending this Saturday writing, processing, or taking care of anyone else's needs.

A magnetic charge is what strings images together from the present to the past.

Coyote persists until I unwillingly rise and wander to the kitchen for my ritual of vitamins, rice milk, cayenne and coffee. Looking around the house at the past night's legacy I slowly begin organizing. By my second cup of coffee, the bed is made, clothing on, and the sun is shining warmly. My morning walk will be in the open space near the post office. Picking up the mail, walking, I could be back in time for what? There are no clues, but Coyote is hanging out close by, trying to find a current story to teach about the Circle of Life. But why today? My mood is rebellious.

The trip to the post office and open space is a five-mile trek.

One of the beauties of living in Colorado is that public land is set aside for preservation and enjoyment of the community. These areas are called open spaces, and usually have hiking trails or dog parks where people can spend free time. I am glad to have such close access from my house to one of these open spaces. I begin driving down a side road wanting to take my time instead of getting on the freeway. I am not ready for prime time driving just yet. As I drive, I think about my landlord Wyn and the little red Jeep with the snowplow that he has for sale. It has low miles and is only a little computerized. Perhaps I could tinker with it when I needed an outlet?

We had last spoken about taking the plow off and driving it around for a test drive. After stopping at the post office, to get the mail, I drive to the open space. On the way, Coyote decides to call Wyn. I am dialing the phone but there are no thoughts behind my fingers. I think as the coffee takes hold, "It would be a nice morning to drive on the mountain roads." Wyn answers the phone. After I speak my request, he says, "Come over right away and help take the plow off." I agree. My walk will have to wait. Coyote is smiling. I feel like, "Here we go." Turning the car around we head towards Wyn's home. When I arrive, Wyn has already started the job. We finish together. Wyn warns me to stay off the main roads, as the license plates aren't current. Agreeing and pulling out of the driveway, I look both ways at the stop sign at the end of the street where Wyn lives. Dream Weaver and I had spoken before I'd left the house. She is awake. Her house is some ten miles over the mountain. I think that I could make it to her house driving around the mountains avoiding main roads and decide to drive her way. Coyote is grinning with excitement and loving this journey.

The late fall colors are dull creating the contrast between the green pines and the dead leaves. Homes dot the mountainsides as the paved road twists and turns through switchbacks. The homes are somewhat attractive with rustic sidings and colors. I notice some strange contrasts between nature's and human's rhythm being revealed. The red Jeep is loud as I drive by these homes. The muffler needs replacing. The loud noise adds a little drama too as I drive by people walking their pet dogs. The Jeep requires all my focus to drive. The short wheelbase adds a rough and quick response to every bump and turn. I think that this is not a cruiser. Humans are playing in their yards as I drive by. The end of the year's growth is done and the Mother Earth is creating her robe for the upcoming winter. Death and change are everywhere. From years of farming I know that water is the robe that seals the Earth while rebirthing. Arriving at Dream Weaver's driveway, I park and walk to the door and knock. She looks at me inquisitively as she opens the door. I invite her by saying, "Let's go for a ride in the Jeep." She looks at me curiously as the words "Okay" came out of her mouth. There is subtle magic in the air.

Leaving her home we start a winding path on the gravel road that has created human "ant trails". We are laughing at the little red Jeep as we chug by posh homes. Dream Weaver asks what I would call this vehicle if I bought it. "Coyote Red" I reply without even hesitating. She looks curiously as she laughs, putting the symbolism together. I watch as she makes the connection. Dream Weaver bursts out laughing before speaking. "Remember the day we went skiing and we watched a Coyote walking across the valley floor towards a herd of Elk?" she asks me. "Yes," I respond. "The Coyote was fooling itself into thinking it was invisible and was red with enthusiasm." The Jeep goes silent as the images we had seen together found there way into our awareness. The sun has brightened by this time and snow covered peaks add an amazing beauty to the morning ride. The drive around the mountains last an hour and seem mostly uneventful except for our talk and the peppy sound of the motor and popping muffler.

The Coyote Red Jeep finds its way back to Dream Weaver's home. We hug and part with an air of unknowingness. As Dream Weaver walks towards her doorway, I watch her curious facial expression. The questions she has are clear. What was that trip all about? Coyote has succeeded!

Dream Weaver:

Later that afternoon, I called Star Blanket and speaking rapidly into the phone, I ask, "What's with Coyote and the Red jeep? I have been sitting at my computer trying to go through a round of edits for this book. It is overwhelming; there are so many topics, so many teachings. I am getting lost in all of the pages trying to get organized according the outline we had prepared.

I am sitting back in my chair and staring at the screen. I keep hearing this voice in my head, 'It's all related, it's all related." I am revisiting the day so far in hopes of seeing where the relation is and to answer why I am getting overwhelmed. I remembered laughing to myself thinking about you banging on the front door saying "Let's go for a ride. I've got the Red Jeep running in your driveway." I know there has to be some relationship. So, 'What's with the Coyote and the Red Jeep?"

Star Blanket responds by laughing. I know at once there is a weaving of a medicine coming. Star Blanket speaks, "Coyote is on my butt this morning! Maybe you tell me what's up with Coyote and the Red Jeep?"

We hang up and I drift back, tilting my chair as far as it will go and cross my outstretched legs upon my desk. I think to myself that this learning to be a Dreamer is sometimes kinda confrontive. Why doesn't he just tell me what's going on, I wonder. After a few moments of feeling self-pity, I relive the morning's journey to see where the pieces will come together. I try to remember as many of the symbols as I can. The images start coming. The morning sun had been melting the snow and tree branches dripped the frozen crystals on the pavement as we drove by. Homes had been visible for only a fraction of a second as most of them were down long driveways behind trees. The standard price, size and architecture were obvious. I continue thinking, "All these people had flaunted their status in the community by identifying with their home. It was their image." I think about the image. There is something gnawing at me and "it is their image" keeps repeating in my head. I go into an inner dialogue. The image is like a character in a movie. The ambiance adds a personality to the human character. After a pause I continue exploring. This image gives security and a sense of belonging. To what I wonder? I am startled out of my dreaming by the phone ringing.

As if reading my thoughts Star Blanket calls. Without hesitation he speaks when I say, "Hello". The image becomes the downfall of many a Seeker, thinking that they can align both realities with different rules for each reality. It can lead to split personalities. There's the artificial world and the natural world. The artificial world seeks to belong by creating the image. The natural world seeks to be efficient because the goal is unknown. It is a great mystery." He says, "Let's talk later." I am getting used to the fact that Star Blanket frequently picks up on my inner reality and I no longer consider it phenomena when he continues my conversation as if we'd been having one out loud. I just put the phone back into its cradle and continue dreaming my dreams.

I remember the drive again. Star Blanket and I had grown quiet while driving past the houses. There is a feeling of scouting and keeping score, like each occupant has medals for rank, like soldiers. The monetary value of the house was the imaged weapon. The mask was architectural, the type of building materials, number of acres, added strength and security to the image. The stronger the image looked, the less the supposed challenges. The homes were a marketing tool of security. I've lived in one of these mountain homes for the past seven years. Even when my life journey was unknown to me at times, my home gives a reference to who I thought I was. I used my home to keep me in the illusion of the security. It has taken me the past three years to illuminate this conflict within myself. I come back to present time, in front of the computer and think, "I'd better go to the grocery store before its too late."

The drive to the store plaza is full of insights as I trace my own fascination with my personal image. I decide to try the newly-opened supermarket in town. This is no ordinary supermarket, this is a supermarket complex. For the past 15 years, here in our little mountain town of Conifer, without a single traffic light, there has only been one town landmark, a small shopping plaza that hosted a Safeway food store and small family owned businesses. The shopping plaza is now under siege since Safeway decided to move its location. I'd been avoiding going there because I knew it was going to be the end of the small town image. I walk into the new Safeway Store. It is like entering another world. Not that I hadn't been in shopping malls before, but this is different. "What has happened?" I remember the ants. "Why?" I wonder.

I walk down the aisles remembering when folks used to say hello. Now the shoppers are like zombies. I have experienced this in some Wal-Marts, people wandering around with shopping carts running into each other, cutting in front of others and being generally very pushy to the elderly and casual shoppers. I ask myself, "Was all of this done in the name of progress because we needed a bigger grocery store? Do we really need 50 spaghetti sauces to choose from? Aren't 5 or 10 enough?" People are aimlessly passing each other, banging into each other's carts, yelling at their kids to get out of the way! When does the sacrifice become enough?"

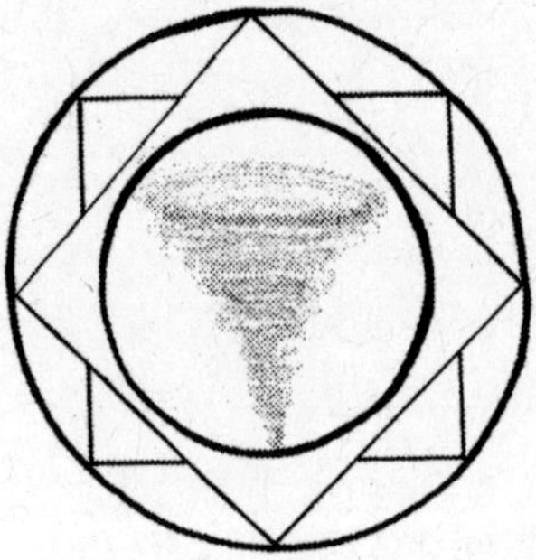

This land used to be a forest inhabited with animals, plants and rocks. The horror becomes a revelation as I look around like I am watching a movie. I have to watch my anger. I am really getting agitated. I think about the image. The image of shopping this way is the shield, a diversion from intimacy with no room to say hi to a neighbor. This is a battlefield. Coyote and the Red Jeep have been insightful teachers this day. I find my groceries and got out FAST. I know during my drive home that Star Blanket is following my journey today and I won't need to fill him in on what has just happened. I pull into my garage, walk upstairs, put the bag of groceries on the counter and call Star Blanket for the review.

Star Blanket answers and again speaks without hesitation. "When humans are centered on our Mother Earth, our life giving mother, they are never affected long by the dark side of an image. This darkness is not evil, however it tricks us by engineering and directing images that lead to comparisons, greed, self-importance and other shortcomings. These create distortions. The images are the weapons that establish rules both spoken and silent. These rules become common law. This is the reality that the Spirit ancestors want us to correct on the planet. It is our destiny as humans. Each individual must find what defines his or her present journey. The children's voices in the wind are counting on it. This journey is the Red Road home."

When we hang up the phone, I know I am at a crossroads and will be making some big decisions in my life. The earlier words spoken by Star Blanket keep ringing in my ear, "There's the artificial world and the natural world." They are beginning to sink in. The time is upon me to open up to what I know is defining my present journey. Instead of beating myself up for some of the choices I have made in the past I am now more interested in how to put down the weapons of the false warrior. I have to let that part of me die so that it will give me room to rebirth. I had no idea a little Red Jeep could be so illuminating. I put my groceries in the fridge. I am exhausted from the day and don't bother eating dinner. I go to my bedroom and relax into the dreamtime looking forward to playing with Coyote.

Chapter 8 - Flower

"Universal Communication is Instant"

Conifer, Colorado 2007 A.D.

Watching, Coyote listens as Star Blanket sings verses from a John Lennon tune. "I am he as you are he as you are me and we are all together. See how they run like pigs from a gun, see how they fly. I'm crying. I am the eggman, they are the eggmen. I am the walrus, goo goo g'joob." Hee Hee the breath of Coyote's snicker scents the air.

Dream Weaver:

Driving to a healing session, which is part of a twenty part series at Star Blanket's home I begin to reflect. Star Blanket calls the healing "an alignment with my Council of Elders." The application today is on Genetic Rivers that meander throughout my body. This session will be on a specific area of visual and audio meridians. Essentially we are going to integrate many of the pieces that we have been working through for the past three years.

I arrived at Star Blanket's office despite the fact that I wasn't feeling so well. My stomach was queasy all morning. I knew from past experience, that what ever was creating this queasy feeling was going to be released from my body during this session. It would be typical that we'd start with some type of discussion or teaching before doing the Medicine Lightwork part of the session. Star Blanket's favorite pattern was starting with a Review, adding Concepts, plus Medicine Lightwork, then Emotional giveaways and finishing with homework assignments. By the end of the session, all my last months' experiences would be related to the new healing.

When I arrived, Star Blanket was sitting in his chair next to his desk and I sat across from him in an office chair. We started talking about this particular set of Genetic Rivers almost immediately. Star Blanket began refreshing my memory. "The last months we have been claiming lost parts of your self by opening the Genetic Rivers. The term "Genetic Rivers" was given in symbolic form, to define different meridians or channels that run throughout the human body that link strands of DNA and RNA. They are like braided hair that twist and wind in a snake like fashion. The Rivers, or meridians, are what the DNA and RNA codes travel through. The Rivers are fluid systems. There are also many infinity patterns that coordinate the body's energy movements. For instance there's an infinity pattern from one foot to the other, and from one ankle to the other, and one knee to the other. The infinity pattern repeats itself all the way to the top of the head. There are many figure eights that connect points throughout the body." Star Blanket explained to me that some foundational teachings from the Dolphin Star Temple identify the meridians and have other terms for sensors. He continued, "Humans have five basic senses; smell, touch, taste, hearing and seeing. Sensors are probes that scout and scan that appear similar to a string of energy fibers, projecting out into the field of energy surrounding the human body. The sensors create a link that can send and receive information. The Genetic Rivers accept or repulse the information that frequently comes in image form. Interpretation of the imaged information is usually instinctual. For example if you look out the window and slow the process down, the first step is the images you see. There are two cars, trees, green leaves, and gravel. The second step is to interpret the image into information. Third is to reject or accept data. It happens very fast." It all made logical sense to me while Star Blanket was explaining. I shifted in my chair a bit, and took a drink of water from the table next to me.

Star Blanket continued explaining the concepts. "The genetic pool is a lake within the human body that contains all the information of your soul's history. The rivers feed information into the lake. When an individual is operating in the zone, all of the fluids are flowing freely from the genetic pool throughout the rivers. The result, that there is absolutely no doubt about anything. The zone refers to when a person is in pure movement with no sense of time. It's a timeless state of being fully present. An example is when you are in yoga posture. There is a point when the movement is fluid and graceful. That is being in the zone." After a brief pause he continued. "The challenge happens when Genetic Rivers release memories from other life times. Once memories are activated, or awakened, you can be living present life circumstances, but be interpreting them from other incarnations because the sensors are receiving the current information and projecting them from the past. For the purpose of the healing today, I'm going to take you through a process of clearing the Genetic Rivers in your cranium of any awakened memories that don't serve you anymore."

"You've had so many experiences of migraine headaches that you have had to take pharmaceutical drugs. You've decided to give up taking those prescriptions. Each time we've gone through a session of clearing Genetic Rivers, the frequency of your migraines has decreased. Do you understand?" he asked. "Yes, I understand. It's just hard to let go of the times that I've gotten headaches with no explanation. I wish I would have been able to realize that there was a reason before taking all of those drugs." Great.

I began daydreaming about how much effort it took, but how good it felt, to thrown away all of my migraine medications months back. Star Blanket started talking again. The words snapped me out of my day dreaming. "The Rivers are usually paired. The Rivers we are going to open today sit in the NW of our medicine wheel system and are located in the head. There are two sets that have a direct link to audio and visual communications. The audio channel is located between the ears lying horizontal, with the center crossing just forward from the center of the brain. The outside curve of the figure eight pattern touches each eardrum, exchanging information as a vibration of sound. The center point intersects, with another infinity pattern that runs from the bottom of the pineal gland, which is just below the Fontanelle, the soft spot on the top of your head. This figure eight extends down towards the pituitary gland which is right behind your third eye, located between your eye brows and in about a half an inch. The two infinity patterns intersect creating a union between audio and visual inputs and outputs. When open, information flows freely. Information will unite or interface with the DNA and RNA codes. This process will have some confusion until the information aligns inside and outside. You will know the alignment when the outside world and you're inside world match." Star Blanket was giving me a big teaching and I was giving him my full attention. He kept speaking. "The purpose of clearing the Genetic Rivers is to remove the distortions of communications both in the spirit and physical realms. Integrity becomes a Teacher when the Rivers are open. Communications are quick, instant, and precise in all circumstances."

Nodding my understanding and excitement to get started, I blurted out "OK." I stood up and moved to lie down on the massage table, covered in colorful cloth. Star Blanket reached over into the closet in his office and pulled another blanket. "Look familiar?" he asked me. I lifted my head to see the apprentice blanket I had given him a few years ago. He placed it on me. It felt comforting to have it on me, keeping me warm. I closed my eyes and realized how much I had grown since the time from when I had originally given this blanket to Star Blanket. He hadn't ever really accepted it. He had said "I am not taking apprentices at this time. You can apprentice to the teachings and the Bundle." I had said, "Okay."

Star Blanket started speaking. "The book we've been writing, Coyote Goes Global, brings a lot of perspectives together. Many questions that you have are going to be answered today. In our writing this book we've gone back in time and we've talked about coded water, councils, and medicine people who seeded your current hunger for knowledge with codes. Those codes are flowing through all humans, animals, minerals and plants. There is a Great Spirit that threads into All that exists on Mother Earth. All has evolved from genetic codes that began from a long time ago. The divine messengers are the air, water, earth and fire."

As the eagle feather brushed across my eyes, a vision appeared. Falling into a foggy dream I came to a dark place. I noticed there was no moon. I watched three or four medicine dancers stepping into a flowing river. Their clothing had symbols of stars, landscapes and giant birds. The dark brown feathers made up wings that were attached to their arms. Head ornaments and beaks stuck out from the dancers' faces. They were all in loin clothes from the waist down. I watched from the banks of the river. The water was shallow coming up to their knees. Each ceremonial costume was personal. The dancers were making a circle and singing as they were moving in the shallow water. I saw a tube of light entering the top of their heads and exiting out the bottom of the spinal column into the water. I realized that what I was watching was the seeding of the water! Weightless stone shapes were floating on the water like flies. As the movement continued, I saw sound from songs, images from costumes and smells from burning sage, all creating the codes. I was watching the feet of the Bird men dancers "fire" the water with their hopes and wisdom for the future. As my eye opened, Star Blanket was smiling as he spoke, "You were there at the Council. Do you see now that you are the Weaver that witnessed at the 1st council and Fire Seeding Ceremony in the early eighth century? Take a few minutes to integrate your vision."

After a short walk around the house I was ready for more. I re-entered the healing room. Star Blanket motioned me to sit and began talking. "The council at Cahokia Mounds wasn't the only council going on around the globe. There were many other groups doing the same thing. Presently on a global scale, memories are being awakened everyday by people who are starting to think for themselves and have who tapped into their spirit selves. They are questioning our leaders; they are questioning our medicines and decisions about social, civil, religious and environment issues. When memories from other lifetimes awaken, humans usually relate the memory to some historical writings that happened in the past. A new approach would be to integrate the memory to current life circumstances. An example would be when in the past they might not have stood up for themselves. Instead of making decisions for themselves, they just went along. So today they carry the same pattern to be followers. Situations like this are happening on a global scale. Although the trickster Coyote is a spirit, and traveling globally, a person can only be tricked when they have something to learn and are not paying attention to the old codes. "Bird men passed on wisdom in forms of music, ceremonies, herbs, stewardship of the forests, and council protocols. Codes from the animals included instincts, highly developed sensory skills and natural links to changing weather patterns. The wisdom came from many tribal medicine societies."

"How am I still tricking myself?" I asked silently. Star Blanket responded hearing my thought, "If you don't clear these Rivers out you could be seduced by the dark side of the Luminary Jumper's skills." That sort of sounds like fun I thought! Star

Blanket continued "Dream Weaver do you remember when you phoned me from the Waldorf Astoria, that ritzy hotel in New York City?" Yes I answered. "You were staying there while working for a legal firm as a technical expert. Consciously your intent was to be there as an expert. You called very sick from a migraine, throwing up in the bathroom. Do you remember?". "Ah Yes, How could I forget?" Star Blanket continued "The Luminary Jumper is a skill of the magician in all of us that can jump realities very quickly. The Magician illuminates whatever the circumstances are. Life can go very dark when the person is not aware of this because they try to understand the present circumstances but there is no fit. Many personality disorders have been created by this dysfunction. At the Waldorf Astoria your spirit started illuminating other realities. The prohibition days and routes through tunnels under the hotel were shown to you. Once we assisted the ghosts of that time to cross over, then your spirit could return to the present time and your head and body healed." My mind raced applying the teaching. This was a huge concept to integrate with the migraine experience I had had. I saw how the Luminary Jumper worked in situations that most people and I considered "difficulties". I could have easily justified my getting sick by saying that it was something I ate, or that I was just getting another migraine. This was a really good example of the DNA coming forward into the present, I thought. We weren't just clearing ghosts from the prohibition days from New York; we also were clearing ghosts from my whole ancestral history back into Europe and the Mediterranean!

As I lay on the table playing back in my head the New York scenario. I saw that Coyote had tricked me into thinking that I had been in NYC to be a technical witness. There were however other realities going on simultaneously. My ancestors had also fought for their rights, as Russians, Jews, and Austrians. In New York I was acting out an OLD war in the legal arena of corporate copyrights. There I was fighting for copyrights, patents and intellectual property just like my ancestors had fought for their land. The legal battle experience was more than I had originally thought. Just then, Star Blanket picked up on my daydreaming and continued, "It was the old active memories within the DNA's, traveling in the watery fluids of your body that you were trying to clear when you were throwing up. Migraines are frozen waters or emotions shrouded in fear. Water is the element that expresses and flows. The Luminary Jumper will go into a dark side, jumping realities to avoid going into the past, in order to escape staying present with the discomfort of accessing the gifts and skills from those disturbing memories. The term Luminary and Jumper are verbs, which are both movements of the Magician archetype. The lyrics of John Lennon, "Imagine if there is no country, I wonder if you can. Nothing to kill or fight for.", came from Star Blanket's mouth as he added, "Sums up your experience of what your ancestors went through huh?"

The room seemed brighter as Star Blanket smiled and a faint odor passed by. "Exactly how I planned" as the sound and odor lingered from Coyote's breath. A retreating echo dimmed the lighting as I heard "They are catching on to my ways."

Thirsty, I reached to get another drink of Awakened Water. The water had been part of a survey program. Over 200 test containers had been sent out to people around the US. Ceremonies had been performed and encoded data was recorded as to the process. We'd recorded a lot of data, the day, time, temperature, Ph, moon day, and we'd filter and bottled the water. The program had been going on for a few months so Star Blanket and I used the water over the course of the sessions on Genetic Rivers. The water had been of great assistance in helping me wake up the DNA memories in my body. My migraines were heredity in my DNA and RNA. It was all fitting together now. I remembered that I had gotten a terrible headache from my teeth. It was like my teeth were on fire and, the fire was spreading throughout my brain. All I wanted to do was find a pair of pliers, to pull my teeth out so that the pain would stop. I had called Star Blanket rather than pulling my teeth.

He was able to see compressed images that were inside my jaw that wound into my head. After many hours on the phone, we worked through each image until they released. Each time, we focused on a specific tooth, it would instantly stop hurting. We went through my entire mouth. One of the images that he questioned was Batman and Robin. I was hurting so much, that I laughed saying "Batman and Robin?" "I used to watch that show all the time after school, why?". What had happened was that many memories of my ancestors, including their battles, had been accessible during my youth. However, I really didn't know what to do with them at that age, so the DNA and RNA codes of the memories of my ancestors got covered up with images from the TV. This would disguise the lesson into an image that my body could assimilate at that time. The images of Batman and Robin's crusades were the way I could relate to my ancestors quest for their uniqueness. Well, the images now were unwinding, and here I was sitting here in 2007, having Batman and Robin flying off my teeth in order to clear the migraine. It would have been comical if it wasn't actually happening before my eyes, and that my headache was leaving. I wondered how the youth of today were doing with all the electronics, video games, TV, and internet, that they were being bombarded with every single day. How much of history was being covered up by images as they burrowed deeper and deeper into their Genetic Rivers. Noticing that Star Blanket was ready to begin again, my inner processing quieted.

Star Blanket put his hands on the sides of my head. I sensed laser-like beams of energy from one ear to the other. He was quiet as my inner dialogue became loud. I had been creating circumstances that diverted my natural instinct towards logic. I keep educating myself out of my inner knowing. That was the issue from my ancestors as well. The conflict between following my knowing and being logical kept showing up in the relationships I chose. I kept picking situations that would create double standards. I would create more confusion until the headaches would get worse and worse. The standards were realities. Each time I was able to clear a set of channels, the confusion would lessen. The unfinished lessons of my ancestors were acting out through my life. God I loved this!

During the Reflection time, Star Blanket was quietly doing energy work on my Genetic River dissolving useless beliefs and smoothing out the geometric structures. We were about to finish the session when I realized that we had a ghost clearing ceremony scheduled in a dental office in a few days. I spoke "I am learning it is all related! Now I knew why the imprinting in my teeth was making way to the surface." Star Blanket smiled, he smudged the room and I got off the table and found my way to the chair.

"Coyote is going global in the spirit world" spoke Star Blanket. Coyote convinces people to go on vacations, to shop, to go to a movie, to read books or maybe to listen to music, as a way of getting their attention away from multiple realities. Every day, water as rain, or snow travels through time and space picking up energy waves from all of our technology, which alters the structure of the water. So now days because we have technology and messages in these energy waves, we have the possibility of also intending love and truth into global ways. Water is being programmed at an alarming rate. Our physical bodies are largely made up of water, so water is the primary element that we need to pay attention to.

The Luminary Jumper is type of "medicine" from the old ways. Modern medicine would call it a "condition". It is a condition and a dynamic where people are avoiding some of the skills and gifts that they naturally have which would help them. Dream Weaver, the truth is that we all are part of the One Spirit – so our races include the Blacks, Yellows, Reds, and Whites. Other parts include the plants, the animals and minerals. We've tricked ourselves as humans into living as a separate species rather than living Oneness. This truth is being revealed as Coyote goes Global."

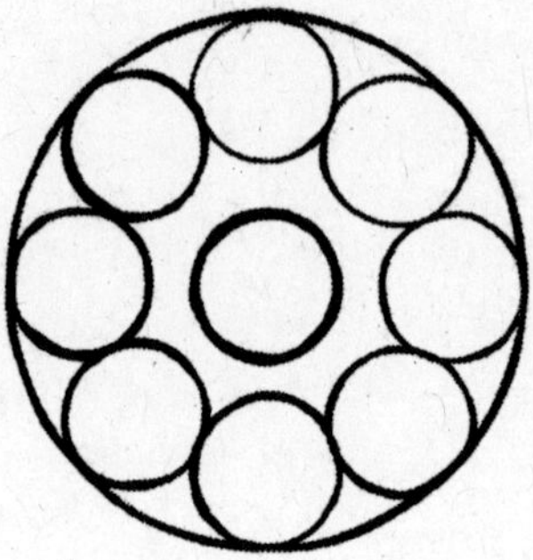

Star Blanket was closing the session. I still had some questions so I asked. "Who are Too Many Red Foxes and Buffalo Heart?" Star Blanket grinned and calmly said "Me". For many years they were separate from me and now they are integrated. I separated in order to dialogue. For you, I must say that you are coming into the medicine of integrity." My facial expression became curious as Star Blanket continued. "I want you to know how proud I am, that you keep your word. Just because your mood changes or you don't feel well, you follow through with what you say. In other words, you continue to be responsible for your actions. You are Dream Weaver and you are the Weaver from the council."

As he spoke, tears welled up in my eyes and started rolling down my face. I knew that he was right. I was able to see this truth now, through my visual channels. Star Blanket and I had been traveling together for some time now and the wholeness of everything was opening up inside me again.

Chapter 9 - Fruit

"Co-Creating has no Future"

Conifer, Colorado, USA in Spring 2007 A.D.

Final Battle - Letting go of the War

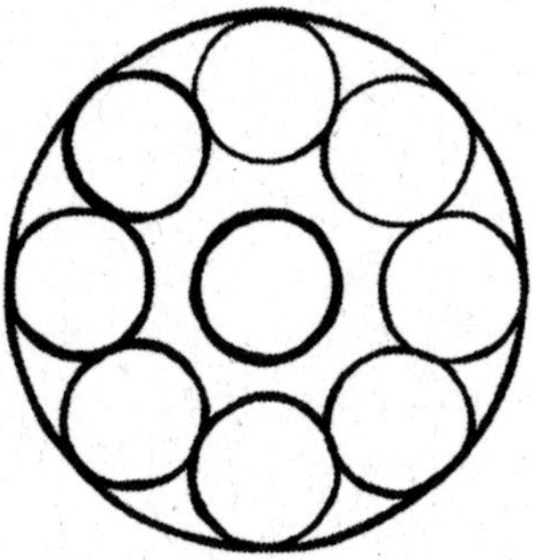

Star Blanket:

The day dream and night dreams are so close that I continue to battle by creating doubt. Acceptance of multiple realities being available every moment is difficult and the challenges are coming from all directions. The "Return" had set in again. The last week's memories of family shame, sexual hungers, and memories of divorce, prison, infidelity and secrets resurfaced. My emotional imprints are spinning out of my body as the purging takes on flu like symptoms. As a new awareness settled in, old memories surfaced and left quickly. My mind runs back and forth from confusion to perfect clarity. I wonder who I am, Guy Gilleshammer, Lone Eagle, or Star Blanket. My quest's end is near and yet the hunt had become my purpose. The years since leaving North Dakota were about gathering my medicine and embodying Lone Eagle's essence, in order to become whole. The cycle of gathering is closing, and yet I hang on. "To what?" I ask out loud.

Grandmother Too Many Red Foxes and Coyote stand near as I

pack my belongings. I am moving soon. The commitments with Spirits I had made in Colorado will complete soon as clients, students and friends are coming into their own link with the Creator. I remember making the commitments when I first traveled the state in 1968. I didn't know what the contracts were, only that I would live in Colorado some day. As household items are packed, the holding matrix of energy flow collapses. Grief begins almost immediately. The phone rings. It is Running Horse. After sharing my feelings, Running Horse talked for two hours about our journey's since meeting in North Dakota. We agreed that we both were seeking a conscious community. With the night dream waiting, I went to bed.

As I lay in bed after praying with my Sacred Pipe, I sense my spirit floating into the dream time. Instinctively I travel deep. As I awaken in the dream, I am sitting in council surrounded by many Elders. They are multi-cultured. Coyote is salivating like an excited puppy and Grandmother is pacing. An old Grandfather motions me to sit on a stump on the south side of a blazing fire. Piñions and sage surround the area giving off fire shadows that dance on shrubs making boundaries. Grandfather Buffalo Heart speaks in a Native tongue that easily translates. "Summers ago your sisters and brothers journeyed to recover knowledge that was lost during wartime. Your quest at the time was in the Bitterroot Mountains. The knowledge is now being held in a Bundle called Renewal Trails Bundle. The knowledge will be needed in coming times. He pointed to a sphere of energy taking form above the fire. The sphere expanded with illustrious colors, like out of a Hollywood movie. The expansion began reflecting images progressing through many years of Earth's history. The sphere began emanating beams of light which stretched across the council's parameters. Each beam was a historical timeline of events that contained imprints of a different species of Earth.

As I watched, my attention focused on a beam of animals. Simultaneously a light stick brushed my leg. I looked up to see

Grandmother Too Many Red Foxes smiling and pointing at a beam of light waves that scrolled human evolution. My eyes also followed old Coyote who was prowling and waiting around the periphery of the circle. Streaks of sparking light were stretched across the sky, and then slowed to a stop, bursting into lightning bolts directed to an area on Earth. Grandmother, standing next to me softly said "Souls are transitioning into spirit selves. Like the Nine Faces," she was referring to a Medicine Wheel from the Renewal Trails Bundle. She turned again to the images. After some time I heard her voice again "This Soul transition to the Spirit Selves has been going on for a very long time on Earth. Remember the Archetypes of Dream Teachers." She went quiet again; I knew the three Archetypal categories to be the Warrior, Lover and Magician. As like being on cue, Grandmother spoke after I had finished this recall. "Every day of a moon cycle, a human experiences a direction of the Nine Faces in conjunction with an Archetype. Watch closely my son." I had never heard her speak to me that way. Tears welled up as I stayed focused on the human events unfolding.

The light beams were scrolling conflicts from many races of people. Bloody battles were showing destruction of land, forests, waters, air and many natural systems of sustainability. Arguments were being shown between men, women, children, religions, governments, and many other forms. My stomach began aching and suddenly I ran to the outside of the Circle and vomited.

Being on all fours, the sound of panting came louder as my focus returned. I looked into Coyote's eyes. Only inches away, Coyote's thoughts seemed to hang in the air. The thought words shouted "When Winged Feet Fire the Water, It Will Be Done." Within minutes I crawled back to the stump in the Circle. Grandmother's hand reached out to my shoulder and rubbed my back caressing the wounds being purged. She spoke "The choice is near for all souls on Earth to choose whether to complete or

Renew with Nature's Ways. The Renewal is living in balance with the feminine and masculine, Creator and Creation. The age of each soul will reveal the intensity of the choice. Elders, adult, youth and infant soul's all reflect the choice to learn from conflict. Elders often have more of a challenge in letting go because the patterning imprints are buried deep in the body."

Again Grandmother went quiet as the light beams showing the human evolution mingled with my current lifetime experiences. Scenes of the Vietnam War, religion, plus deception of government leaders flashed on the light beam along with the blending of cultural foods, technology, products and philosophies. Too many memories flashed throughout my body collapsing my focus. I passed out in the dream!

The night's dream lingered as I began the day packing and cleaning up my home. The spring of 2007 was in full swing. My time in Conifer, Colorado was closing. As I wrapped pictures and dream shields, memories of relationships came to me. The decision to come to Conifer began with meeting Night Hawk Woman; we had talked about writing a book called "Grandmother's Return." A discussion followed with my sons Ian, Micah and Jacob on a Christmas day afternoon in Sandpoint, Idaho. Our agreement was that I would go on one more adventure to write about the Métis Medicine Ways before planting roots and being in community. That adventure was coming to completion by embodying the medicine of Star Blanket. The time to complete my agreement with my sons had arrived. Standing Flame had moved to Conifer also. He found love with Thunderbird Woman at one of the training lodges. Micah, Dream Weaver and I would travel to Hawaii at the end of July for their marriage. We were all to be part of the wedding party. Dream Weaver would be a bridesmaid, Micah best man and I would officiate the wedding. Chandra, who wrote the article on Peruvian Shamanism from Sun Valley Idaho, had moved to Kaui, Hawaii near where the wedding was planned! Dream Weaver and I had met her while researching the water in

Southern Idaho. Coyote had been a master trickster on that trip. Meeting again could open up another mystery.

Dream Weaver settled in to her own path of Shamanic studies while promoting her technology company's sale. Her expertise in software technology has opened many doorways. Most of her visions have come true and the journey of accepting her destiny had begun. Her plan was to join me in Durango next year for researching and practicing the Ways of Nature. Coyote would be a powerful ally as her software was to go international.

Continuing to pack, my thoughts jump into the future. I am moving to the Durango area of Colorado and letting go of the war. I will continue there to complete my life's purpose manifesting a tribe like the one I longed for from a long time ago. The Spirit of the water will find us all. These thoughts gently pass as snow falls softly outside the window. My eyes close as a day dream calls me in. I fall asleep in the chair. Grandmother approaches and speaks without words "The Warrior Shame is the subtle emotional issue that humans face. With so many lifetimes of feeling bad, and yet not knowing what to feel bad about. Guilt is when you feel emotionally bad for behaving against your values. This can be forgiven by a change of behavior. Shame is when you feel bad and cannot connect the feeling to a behavior. Therefore shame is a projection of guilt from another person or group. Only personal accountability can end this transference of responsibility that is at the root of creating shame. The Warrior's need for structure is rooted within conflict and conflict will be repeated, unless personal responsibility is realized. The competitive behavior and choices of capitalism will eventually illuminate the insanity.

The current human conditions reflect shame in every area of Earth, like polluting and endangering waters, species, and forests. Covering up the residues of destruction to create cannot continue. Coyote's purpose is to reveal the disguises of Warriors addicted to conflict be they in business, religions, governments, or personal relations, with animals, plants and Earth herself. Unless, we change and unite to rebalance the planet, the Warrior will continue a path of destruction to justify the abuse of Earth's resources. All inhabitants of the Earth have created the current out of balance ecological systems on earth and all inhabitants are accountable. Co-existing is the way The Great Spirit intended. Co-creating will become obsolete as personal accountability becomes a principle of living. This is the common purpose of current incarnations." Grandmother's image evaporated as she walked away.

Awakening in the lazy boy chair I remember Grandmother's words. Half asleep I padded my way to the bedroom and slipped under the medicine blanket. Almost instantly I was Dreaming again with Grandmother when I heard the words of an Elder. "Coyote is learning to swim and Mother Earth is mostly water!" I sat straight up in bed as the voice became mine. It was the Elder speaking! Where would Coyote's next adventure be?

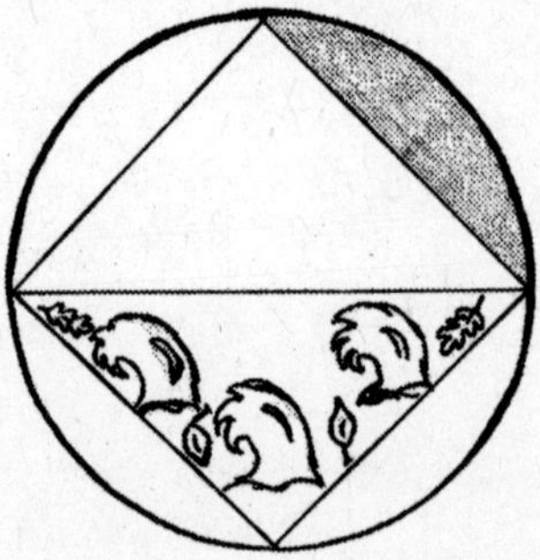

About the Authors

Star Blanket - Born in 1954 as Guy Gilleshammer, Lone Eagle aka Star Blanket is a mixed blood of Cree/Métis and Norwegian decent. His vision quest trail began in North Dakota/Minnesota near the Canadian border as a youth working the land on the family farm. After an intervention from the spirit world in 1983, he began several paths of self-discovery. In the early 1990's, the family farming lifestyle and business closed after several years of drought and corporate influences. Personal studies with the bible, therapeutic foster care, human services, Sweat Lodges, spiritual healing and a hunger for answers continued, when the Elder Eagleheart came into Guy's life from the Turtle Mountain Chippewa reservation. Given the Spirit Name Lone Eagle, the integrating of Earth's secrets and the quest for peace accelerated. Studies added the transformational process of Spiritual healing with Amorah Quan Yin of Mt Shasta California, Sweet Medicine Sundance Teachings and assisting leadership with Metis Medicine Ways in Sandpoint, Idaho. Today, after co-creating two series of educational and alternative medicine training programs, some 3000 healings, 300 training lodges and several ceremonial retreats, work has begun on pioneering new levels of change through venues of Awakened Water, writing and music while maintaining a private practice of consulting. Another quest includes designing, researching and applying a model that interfaces the business world with the ways of Mother Earth. Lone Eagle aka Star Blanket is now Keeper of the Renewal Trails Bundle and resides in the Durango, Colorado area.

Dream Weaver of the Crane's Flight - For 38 of the past forty something years, I walked this world as Sue Spielman. My path has taken me from being born and raised on Long Island in New York, to spending many years in the Boston area and eventually making my way to the mountains of Colorado. Many of those years were spent in the world of high tech as a Software Engineer whose experience has included designing and architecting systems for companies around the globe, authoring six books in technology and business, and speaking on emerging technology both domestically and internationally. A serial entrepreneur, Sue has experience at numerous startups, including her own consulting and high tech companies. She has played all roles within a company, including executive management. After many years of traveling around the world and exploring various spiritual paths including Judaism, Buddhism, and Yogic, she stepped onto a path that involved weaving ancient indigenous knowledge with the Ways of Nature. This path, called Braided Traditions, has been calling her throughout her entire life, only she didn't know it. In 2003, Sue began studying, healing sessions, and working with Eagle Star Blanket, and became an apprentice to the ways of the Renewal Trails Bundle. Shortly thereafter, she became Dream Weaver of the Crane's Flight and took on the responsibility of the medicine being revealed to her from within. Dream Weaver is an assistant, and apprentice to the movement of Braided Traditions and provides a lens and a bridge from the world in which most businesses operate and the world of the teachings of Nature.

Glossary

Ah Ho is an expression used to signify understanding, completions and honoring of the moment.

Akashic Records is any container that holds recorded experiences. Sometimes called a Book of Life and spirit library, records are kept in symbols, codes or other forms of language.

Alchemy is the process of chemical changes during a conversion of energy from one form to another. Shamanic ceremonies are designed to co-create certain alchemies for transformation, assisting change.

Archetypes are the original anchor of the spirits terrains of learning. Three Archetypical spirit categories are Warrior, Lover, and Magician that are explored in the Renewal Trails Bundle. These archetypes encompass many lifetimes of experiences.

Assemblage Spin is a movement of perception, viewing point of reference or advancement in levels of maturity.

Astral and Astral Travel are terms used to describe the realms and routes a spirit travels. For instance when a human dreams during the day or night, the spirit travels through time and space which is called Astral realm.

Aura is the reflecting energy field after light travels through a substance grounding the circuit. The emanation or energy that radiates from a body's chakra system.

Awakened Water is water that has been structurally changed by a ceremonial and conscious process.

Banishing is a commanding of a space to be in alignment with intent.

Bladder Bag is a bag made from a bladder of an animal to contain and preserve liquids and perishable foods.

Blanket and Apprentice Blanket is a traditional gift of honor. It is also used to symbolically represent a contractual agreement.

Bundle refers to a containment of knowledge in various forms. It's a traveling library that stores information on plants, history, ceremonies etc.

Ceremony is a process, that alchemy occurs within the steps and another level of awareness is experienced and witnessed.

Chakras are vortexes of rotating wheels within the body that radiates energy through the body creating a field of energy called an aura.

Circle is a gathering that is arranged in a circular fashion for maximum efficiency and containment.

Clairvoyance is the sensory ability of seeing other forms of light waves beyond the physical visual spectrum.

Clan usually refers to a grouping or pod of like forms exploring the same way of living. A social architectural unit of a society, that includes several villages, bands that share common interests, purpose or family bloodline. They are usually recognized by a similar totem, name or location.

Cocoon of Light refers to a container of gridded energy waves. Cocoons of light contain layers of information in one's aura.

Creating with the Moon – see appendix 'Creating with the Moon' teaching

Crystal Medicine is the usage of crystals as a tool to amplify, transfer and transform. Crystals can be programmed for specific intents.

Cyclic Readings are daily, moon, seasonal and yearly divination readings that follow the Thirteen Moon Steps of Creating illuminating the terrain for gathering learning and conscious imprinting of movements. See contact information for details.

Dolphin Star Temple is a non-profit church set up to receive and transmit information from the Pleiadian Emissaries of Light. The Dolphin Star Temple is physically located in Mt. Shasta, CA.

Day Dreaming is the expansion of conscious thoughts through time and space during day light.

Divine Feminine is a title that refers to the receptive energy within the universe.

Divine Masculine is a title that refers to the active energy within the universe.

Dreamer is a Shamanic title that defines a mastery of skills to extend through time and space into alternate realities.

Dreams are the expanding of awareness within time and space.

Fire Keeper/Fire Chief is a title given to a person that has a special relationship to fire and uses that skill to assist others.

Fluid Systems are any routes that use liquid to transport information from one location to another.

Genetic Rivers are the channels in the physical body through which fluid containing DNA and RNA travels.

Genetic Structure is a shaping or framing, that includes etheric platonic solids creating a container for images of experiences to compress into a symbol.

Ghost is the spirit that has separated from a physical body which is lost in another dimension or realm of existence.

Grandmother's Return Lineage Pipe is the Sacred Pipe dedicated to the return of the divine feminine principle into daily lives. It unites with the Divine masculine principle.

Grid usually refers to a geometrical shape with many angles of light that construct a framework.

Journey includes the stages and steps taken from one position to another. The steps can be physical, emotional and/or spiritual.

Ka Channels are the body meridians through which energy flows. They are channels of energy that allows a spirit to anchor more fully into the body.

Kachina Dancing is an experience of acting out in a physical form, a spirit in order to transform, interpret or reclaim personal power.

Kachina Dolls - refers to figurines of dolls that are decorated to represent the spirit of an energy form or movement.

Karma is a term that defines the revolving symbolic images of experiences cycling through time and space.

Keeper of the Ways is a title given to any form that is designated to hold or keep records.

Kiva is an earthly lodge usually dug into the earth. A Kiva used for many purposes including praying and re-birthing.

Lessons are tests and goals that a human creates in order to master situations or a level of consciousness.

Lightworker refers to any form that harnesses light waves and directs the energy towards their working purpose.

Lineage Pipe is a sacred pipe that is directly connected to a Bundle of Knowledge and or a Tradition with ancestors that have journeyed a similar trail.

Lodge is any gathering of people who share intent.

Lover Archetype is the Archetype that allows all lessons and incarnations to exist. Open communication is the way of the Lover, which makes all things possible.

Longhouse is the term used to describe a physical structure for used gatherings. Longhouse's can be homes, churches, community centers, used for ceremonial and religious purposes.

Magician Archetype is the archetype that creates a path or forum of resolution. "Integrity" of energy movement is the way of the Magician.

Mah-Kuh-Ney is a mixed cultural word that describes the zone when a human is in the purest moment of energy movement with out thought or a sense of time.

Mask is a projection or presentation of a personality that cleverly adds mystique or illusions to the spirit purpose.

Medicine is a gift that assists in clarity, healing, purpose or well being. The term Medicine relates to the spirit's ability to heal, not the practice of allopathic medicine.

Medicine Drum is a drum that has been blessed for providing medicine. See Medicine Lightwork.

Medicine Lightwork is a term that defines the directing of light and sound waves that will produce a medicine. Medicine is used here as the result of discovering truth.

Medicine Wheel is a model, hologram of circular design, experience and represents all the aspects of life. Every wheel is built with four elements: water, earth, air and fire. A medicine wheel is a containment of energy that provides a mirror reflection of one's creation.

Mesa is an altar like setting that is used as a sacred space. Mesa is a flat table top area of earth found in southwest areas of the US.

Métis Medicine Way is a path and way of life that a Mixed Blood lives embracing and weaving techniques, knowledge, and culture. These experiences have developed into a tradition, lineage and community.

Milky Way Experience refers to nine levels of mastery, through incarnating within the Milky Way Galaxy.

Moon Medicine – see appendix 'Creating with the Moon' teaching

Mystery School is a controlled environment for advanced learning and knowledge, usually including ceremonies of initiations.

Mystic is a seeker and practitioner of spiritual esoteric traditions.

Natures Teachers – see appendix 'Creating with the Moon' teaching

Night Dreaming is the expansion of consciousness thoughts through time and space during night.

Nine levels of mastery refer to a purpose of reclaiming and embodiment of nine spirit selves that the soul has divided within the Milky Way constellations that sustain life.

Nine Faces refers to spirit personalities that are in direct relationship to each human.

Parallel Lives are the lives in different realms that our spirit inhabits.

Persona is a theme that our personality operates within, often defined by themes, stories and how we entertain ourselves (i.e. western, drama, adventure, romance).

Pleidian refers to light waves from the Pleidian constellation, also known as the Seven Sisters. Beings of this parallel existence guard and harmonize our self concepts.

Platonic Solids are basic geometrical building designs that are the foundation of nature.

Portal is an energetic entry or exit point for consciousness to move through.

Pouring often refers to a person delegated to bless or assist prayers with water.

Renewal is the transitional movement from the silence to the waking state that is the time of awakening from the sleeping dream to the waking dream. Renewal is the clarity of movement from one cycle of experience to the next cycle of experience.

Renewal Festival is an annual gathering that celebrates common relationships such as purpose, bloodlines, crafts and nature.

Renewal Trails Bundle is a library of knowledge being held in a container.

Return refers to the movement of a spirit returning to an internal place.

Rite of Passage is an 'accepted' entry from one lower form of consciousness into a higher form of consciousness. This transition of movement is the passage and the right, which has been earned!

Running Rocks is the task of handling stone people from one location to another. Stone people are the spirit of the rocks.

Sacred Fire is a fire that has been impregnated with a specific intent.

Sacred Law is a synergy of energy which governs principles, so all moves in a co-existing way.

Sacred Hoop refers to the symbolic circle that unites four colors of people. Red, Yellow, White and Black and all colors that are mixed.

Sacred Pipe is made with a stem and bowl representing male and female qualities, decorated with symbols of all worlds for co-creative purposes. Tobacco and/or herbs are placed in the pipe with intents and purposes. The smoke carries the intents to the Creator and All that is.

Sacred Sexuality is consciously uniting. It is the reunion of separated forms that have a spirit. This union creates an increase in life force energy by eliminating separation!

Sandpainting is an arrangement of symbolic painting on sand that aids as an interpreter, map, language and portal for spiritual exchanges into the physical realms.

Seeker is a person that quests knowledge to answer questions.

Shaman is a seeker that practices the art of being in relationship to Universal movements.

Shamanism is an art of metaphysical and physical practices, which explores all time-space possibilities and the relationships to Nature's rhythms within all forms.

Sigil is a symbol created for a specific magical purpose. A sigil is usually made up of a complex combination of several specific symbols or geometrical figures each with a specific meaning or intent.

Smudge is a combination of dried plants that when burned produces a smoke to surround images unseen and seen. Smudging is used to clean and neutralize the energies of a physical space.

Sorcery is the ability to source the force within and direct the force towards an intended goal.

Societies are clans or communities which share common interests. Societies, subgroups or committees' research, study, practice or educate for specific reasons. Examples would be a university has a Law Society, Medical Society or Business Society. Circles within the Circle.

Soul is the individuated part of the Creator, within the animal and human bodies. The Soul is the part of us that contains memory. It is the part that lives forever. The Soul is the infinite identity that carries the image of the Creator and Creation.

Spirit is a sacred part of the self which is not limited by the physical body. A soul divides into multiple spirits, each containing memory of the others. One of the gifts is scouting function both inside and outside of the body.

Spirit Name - is a name given that creates a relationship to the plants, minerals, animals and humans.

Sky Woman's Web is map of stars with imaginary lines connecting each star.

Sweat Lodge is a nest shaped structure turned upside down used for birthing, protection and purification. It is one of Nature's churches.

Talking Stick is a decorated part of the standing nation, commonly know as a tree. Its symbols connect all worlds. In a circle, the person holding the Talking Stick has the privilege of speaking. This ancient tool provides a sacred space of respect and trust.

Thunderbirds are the Higher Selves of the animal world. Thunderbirds are the symbolic spirits of all weather patterns and ecological movements.

Totems are allies/messengers from any of the Four Worlds of Mother Earth who provide an energy message. The Four Worlds are Plant (south), Mineral (west), Animal (north) and Human (east).

Tribal Tree is a blueprint, shaped like a tree that is imprinted with memories of historical lineage.

Truth are qualities that give movement to energy and the images attached.

Turtle Island is a name for the North American continent because of its is shape similar to a turtle. In some oral traditions of indigenous people, the turtle had a vital role in saving North America from the great flood. The shell of the turtle also records the movement of the 13 moons of a lunar year.

Vision Quest is a ceremonial process experienced in and with nature by which one seeks a vision. One gazes into the unknown mystery for life purpose, direction and clarity.

Warrior Archetype is the archetype that illuminates the terrain of learning and the light and dark of situations. "Honor" is the way of the Warrior.

Wheel of Purpose is any circle of any form that seeks/explores to answer the questions WHY? WHERE? WHEN? HOW? Therefore the wheel/circle has purpose! The purpose is an intent that is aligned with Sacred Laws.

This glossary was compiled for clarifying the meaning of the Renewal Trails Bundle of Shamanic Teachings. No claims are being made as to the use of these terms for any other culture or tradition.

Appendix - Creating with the Moon

Taught by Star Blanket

The moon was full as Dream Weaver and Star Blanket finished the writings for "Coyote Goes Global". The Moon is one of the strongest choreographers of energy movement and rhythms of the human energy system on Earth. This can be understood by the enormous amount of water in our bodies and on Mother Earth. The Moon's and Earth's orbit creates an energy field of opposites called duality. Water is moved from one point to another, called Tide when referring to the ocean, and carries information throughout. A similar effect takes place in humans, plants and animals.

This story was drafted to outline the twenty eight day cyclic movements of a solar year. There are thirteen movements of the thirteen moons in a solar year, each being approximately twenty eight days long. Our goal is to show the correlation of a longer orbit to a shorter cycle. There is predictability to the steps of the cycle.

The book chapters are outlined from zero to nine with four remaining chapters that will likely be experienced by the reader on their own schedule. The last four steps are called Return, Compost, Silence and Renewal. All thirteen steps are listed below with their respective seasonal teacher.

Our final teaching of this journey will be to outline and give some parameters to the steps on Creating with the Moon. Also the last four stages of Return, Compost, Silence and Renewal can assist many readers with some possibilities they may experience as a completion with this process.

All stages are a continuous movement from Zero and back.

Creating with the Moon

1. Seed - An assemblage of layered intents. The seed itself is an energy sphere of intents. The element of fire will ignite the

awakening. For humans this can be passion. Spring time of Earth is the teacher when the Father Sun ignites the seeds from the last cycle. Seeding is the final action of this stage. During the previous cycles of nature, a selection process has determined the placement and types of seeds that will germinate. Humans must also go through this selection process as to what intents to ignite. If the intents are new, humans must be absolutely clear. Seeds from the previous cycle often lay quietly in the subconscious. The seed can be ignited by fire from a cellular memory and is expressed through images associated with ideas, goals, projects and purpose.

2. Union - This is the act of uniting physical matter (earth) to seeds of intent. When the seeds of intent are united, two qualities are present. There is both an active (male) and receptive (female) principles of energy. By the union of these two principles vibration is created and radiated. The more these qualities are present the deeper the availability of hereditary codes of RNA and DNA. Light waves penetrate the substance of Earth. Mineral world, plants, animals and humans are born out of elements and genetic codes.

3. Egg - An egg is formed by the addition of Seed (intents) and Union (resources) . This third stage is a container like a butterfly's cocoon that gives form and is a symbolic image of manifestation. When I view the mountain meadows in late spring there is an ambiance that predicts the rest of the growing season. This ambiance is the egg's aura. For folks that work with gardens or farming crops this sensation is noticeable within a short duration after the seeding and adequate watering. Humans experiencing transformation during this stage will have a view point of the hills and valleys ahead along with the courses of growth available. The feelings of wholeness of the egg stage gives motivation and a protective quality like being pregnant.

4. Sprout - From the egg stage, plants sends scouts called sprouts into the elements of Earth seeking the resources for the

growth cycle. From these resources a determination will be made as to the course of growth. Nature's cycle of late spring to early summer reflects the intelligence of the resources available. The mountain meadow grasses have made this determination and can be understood by the length of the sprouts. For example a dry year will have shorter sprouts. Whether it be a project or personal transformation, a human's course of living becomes predictable by the attention given to this stage. As in nature, an accurate assessment of the reliable resources determines the support while creating the latter stages.

5. Root - Once the scouting sprouts have determined the resources needed the roots are established for feeding elements into the growth cycle. This movement usually goes deep into the earth and spreads out like a web. This foundation sets up the stability and flexibility of the growth cycle. For an example if I try to pull out a weed in mid-summer after the roots are set I will find it much more difficult than in spring time. In human business models the terms networking, out sourcing, and collaboration are the rooting phase. For projects and personal transformation the Root stage applies to creating a circle of resources that supports the course of action and intents chosen.

6. Trunk - This stage in the plant world happens after the roots are set and feeding from the earth. Once the network of feeding is established, the growth accelerates stretching for resources above the ground. There is no goal motivation with the plant world other than to be efficient. The growth reflects the beauty by nature's standards. Nature's standard is efficiency. This stage reflects the same beauty in human growth as well. Nature's standard of efficiency is the beauty of being within the alignment of resources available. No more or less. Projects that are motivated by an end goal can benefit by having participants enjoying the journey and having them be attentive to the efficiency of the previous stages and following ones. The trunk is a growth that is quiet and steady. Very often it is a boring movement for those

folks needing thrills and various stimulations.

7. Budding - This stage is not consistent with the yearly seasonal cycle of nature. Some of the plant world reveals this mystery within various shorter cycles. Examples are flowers and trees. The budding is a result of two forms being in harmony. The first three stages Seed, Union, Egg followed by Sprout, Root and Trunk are the forms representing the Feminine and Masculine principles of energy movement. The harmonizing of the Budding sets in motion a presentation that births the ingredients and codes from the learning thus far. When humans reproduce a child, the child contains DNA and RNA from both parents plus codes from their soul's many lifetimes. If we use these stages as a guideline of the creation process the child is a presentation of all the previous stages. The child will contain all the images of the experiences in a coded form. Human projects are very similar when you look for all the images that went into the manifestation. Budding is the labor stage of the presentation.

8. Flowering - The Flowering is the announcement to all of Earth's watchers. The plant world teaches this by the word itself. Flowering is the presenting of innocence, willingness, vulnerability with an array of colors, fragrance and sharing. Like a newborn child of humans, the flowering models the beauty of creation's gifts. This coming out can have erratic movement that depend upon the environment. For the plants it can be current weather or animals feeding. Projects can experience applause or criticism. For the human children, the same challenges can come from conditions and those people who greet their arrival. In all three examples the reception is influenced by the ease or dis-ease of the previous stages.

9. Fruit - The fruit is the ninth step that signals a change in the cycle's pattern of growth. This ninth stage is chaotic as the packaging of data occurs. The ripening of a fruit tree is an example of this stage. The growth cycle quits expanding movements. The ripening of the fruit is the most visible motion

while the rest of the tree begins retracting. The fruit undergoes exposure to insects, animals and weather while preparing to be converted into other energy forms. The data is compressed into the fruit as preparation for the Return. For humans it is the stage of creation that breaks the current pattern or rhythm. The fruit will contain the imprinted codes of the learning cycle and the lesson itself.

10. Return - This movement is reflected at the end of summer when leaves, fruits and nuts return to the ground below. For humans a similar movement happens after a peak in energy intensity. The spirit has gathered information from the progressive acceleration of energy and will bring the information into the body by way of an entry point below the navel. The information is dropped into a set of geometric figures and from there the information is radiated out into the energy field for accessibility. The information is distributed throughout the body by water for an equal radiation. During this stage symptoms of laziness, disorientation and bargaining may occur. The depth is usually determined by the range of emotions the person is capable of. The bargaining symptom is because the person's ego is trying to reinstall the personality's old way of operating and the information of the last growth peak does not yet fit. The movement will have an inner conflict until a subtraction of some limiting imprint occurs. Erratic decisions and chaotic behaviors are often a result until a circuit opens. Then with the space open the new information will find its home and the next step will begin. In a fast paced lifestyle, this step is often overlooked and as age progresses the consequences show up in peoples lives. The most efficient way of navigating through this stage is by honoring the time it takes. If a lifestyle is full of schedules and deadlines, then having unstructured time to do preparatory tasks can assist the depth of the process.

11. Compost - Once the imprint of new information has found a home, the composting begins. It is like a digestive process where

a separating of data takes place. This step or stage is reflected clearly in nature when the Return nears completion. In colder climates, the killing frosts have left most of the plant world bare. In warmer climates the contrast is more subtle. The Return completes with the Mother Earth placing a robe of rain, snow or other forms of water that creates a seal to the land. The Composting stage then has little interference from external events. Humans can expect symptoms of energy spurts. Spurts can be more or less energetic. These highs and lows also will apply to purpose, decisions and personal needs. For humans the length of composting can vary depending upon the lifestyle and the degree of changes in lifestyle required from an experience. This stage is a great teacher of the law of conservation.

12. Silence - Nature is the ultimate teacher of this stage. It is the quiet of quiet... just being! When growing up in North Dakota, a walk in the woods during this stage brought the sound of my thoughts into awareness. I could hear myself talking. This is the resting after rebirth. For humans this stage is full of symptoms. They can range from having intense dreams, passion, purpose, anxiousness, and restlessness. All of these symptoms are a precursor to beginning a new cycle and are usually cut off before starting with diversions, distractions or just a crash of inspiration. It is a time of resting before an awakening and humans can benefit by just being rather than having to perform or prove themselves valuable. It is a pulse of soft power from the Mother's love for just existing.

13. Renewal - The movement of Renewal is an awakening from the sleeping dreamer of nature. The elements of fire, air, Earth and water will slowly show movement in colder climates with gentle drips, warm soft comforts while branches on trees begin to soften. Grasses will start greening signaling the changes ahead. The movement is guided toward the flexibility and durability needed for spring. For humans this is a time of preparations. Day dreaming, imaging the resources needed for goals and

researching of ideas can be symptoms of the Renewal taking place within the body. A good way to understand this stage is the period between sleeping and waking up where you are not awake or asleep. This is the Renewal stage! For best recall of the dreams during the Renewal, a slow but deliberate movement can facilitate the remembering. This can be done like slowly making breakfast in the morning allowing the speed of movement to pick up the pace as integration occurs. Mother Earth teaches this movement when moving from winter to spring as she gently increases the elements song. An example is the sun's heat increases causing the water to begin melting.

Appendix – Sphere Sigils

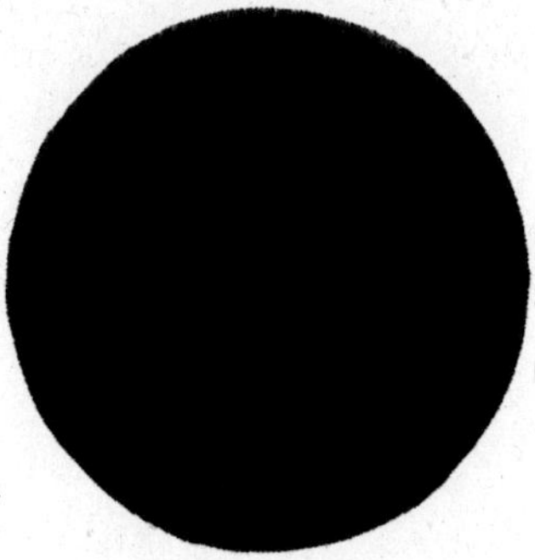

Great Mystery Sphere

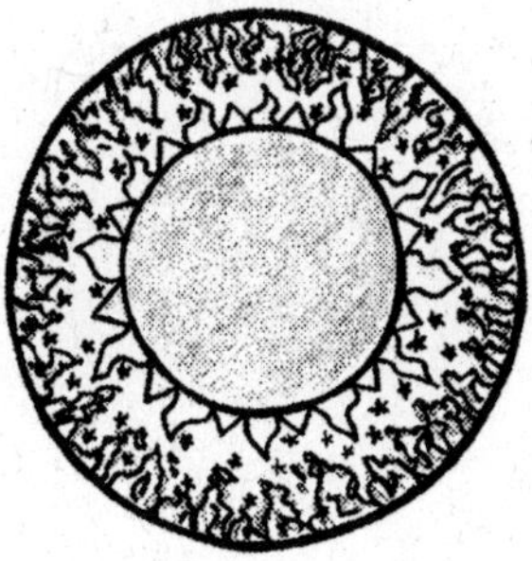

Sphere of Stars and Suns

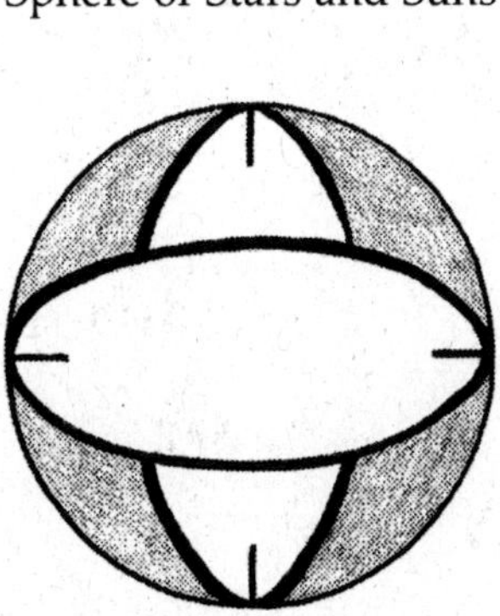

Sphere of Minerals

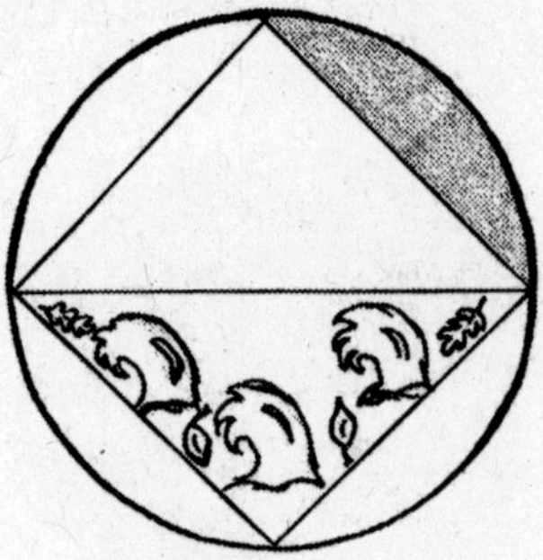

Sphere of Plants

Sphere of Animals

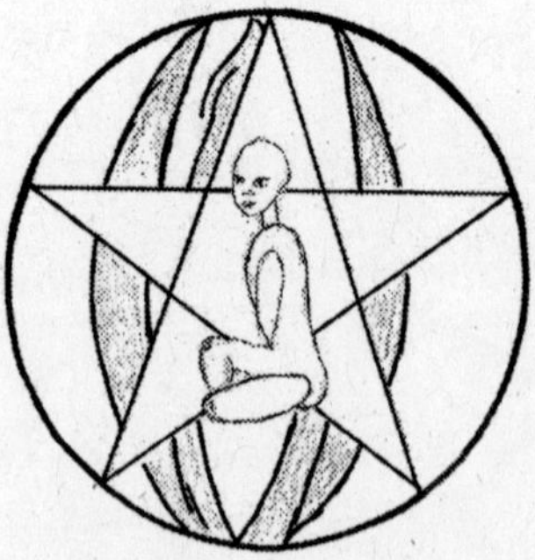

Sphere of Humans

Sphere of Duality

Sphere of Symbols

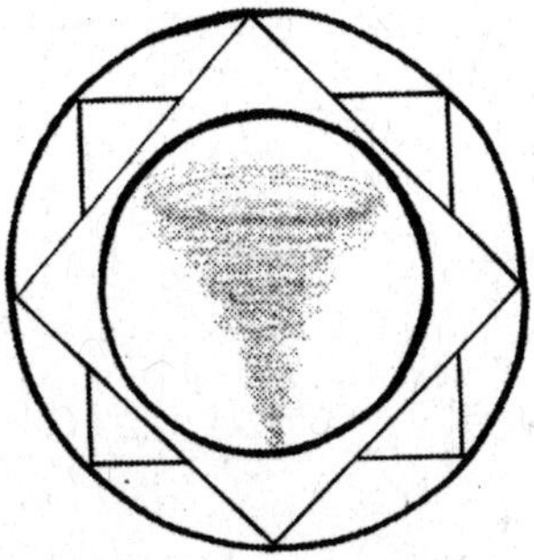

Sphere of Cycles

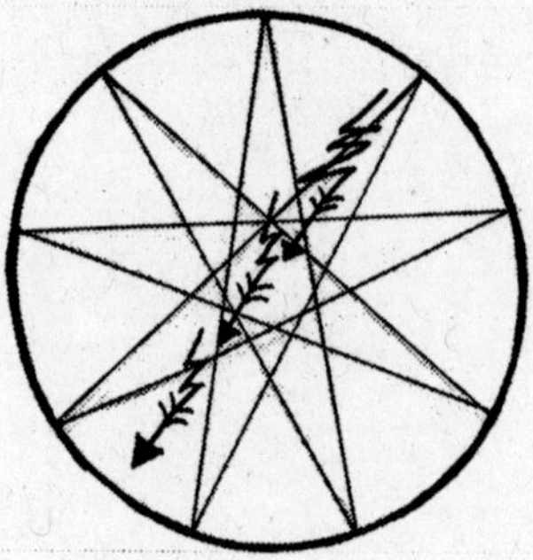

Sphere of Regeneration

Sphere of Wisdom

For additional information regarding teachings, lodges, cyclic readings and events visit Braided Traditions at http://www.braidedtraditions.com or email at info@braidedtraditions.com